PIANO / VOCAL / GUITAR

SARA BAREILLES
AMIDST THE CHAOS

T0084206

ISBN 978-1-5400-5303-9

HAL•LEONARD®

Visit Hal Leonard Online at
www.halleonard.com

Contact us:
Hal Leonard
7777 West Bluemound Road
Milwaukee, WI 53213
Email: info@halleonard.com

In Europe, contact:
Hal Leonard Europe Limited
42 Wigmore Street
Marylebone, London, W1U 2RN
Email: info@halleonardeurope.com

In Australia, contact:
Hal Leonard Australia Pty. Ltd.
4 Lentara Court
Cheltenham, Victoria, 3192 Australia
Email: info@halleonard.com.au

CONTENTS

FIRE

Words and Music by
SARA BAREILLES

*Recorded a half step lower.

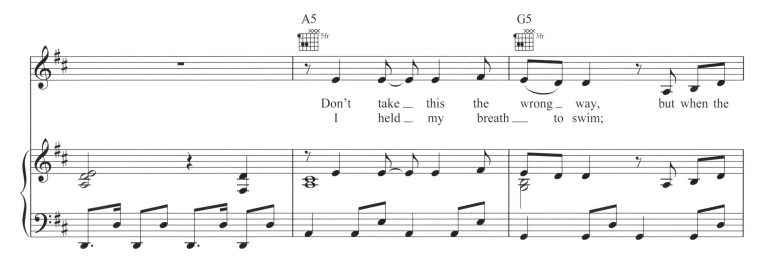

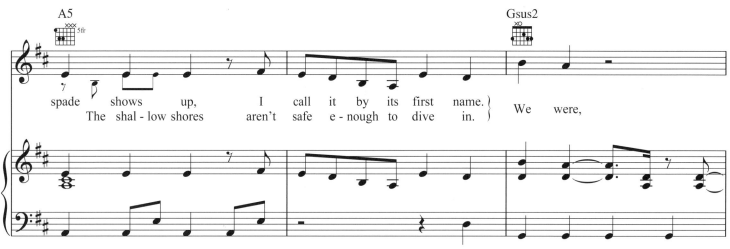

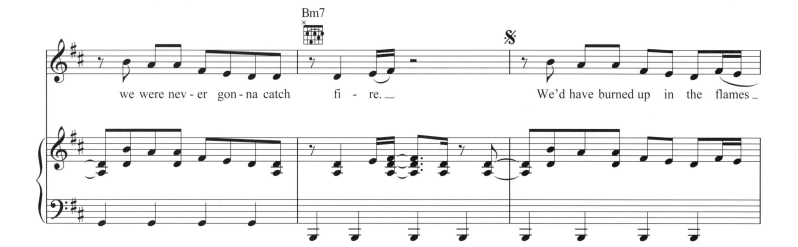

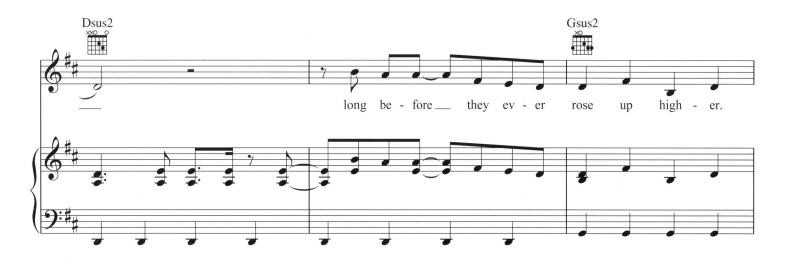

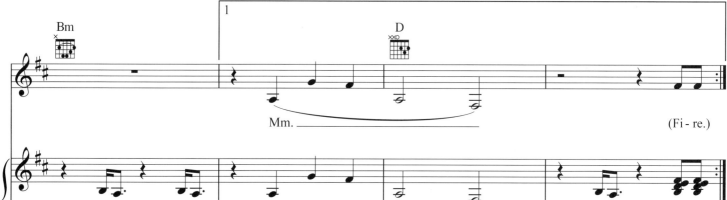

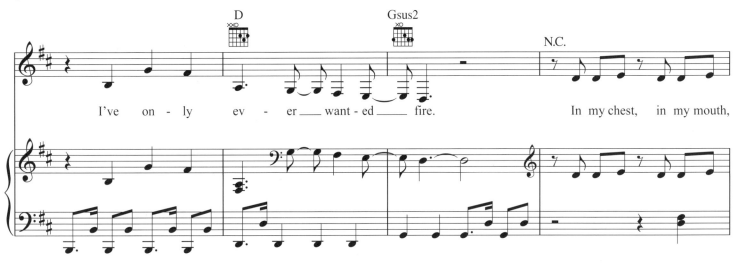

I've on - ly ev - er __ want - ed __ fire.

In my chest, in my mouth,

on my tongue, in my mind, in my soul, so my lungs __ can breathe __ in fi -

- re. ____

D.S. al Coda

CODA

fi - re, fi - re.

IF I CAN'T HAVE YOU

Words and Music by SARA BAREILLES,
AARON STERLING and EMILY KING

*2nd time, substitute Cm.

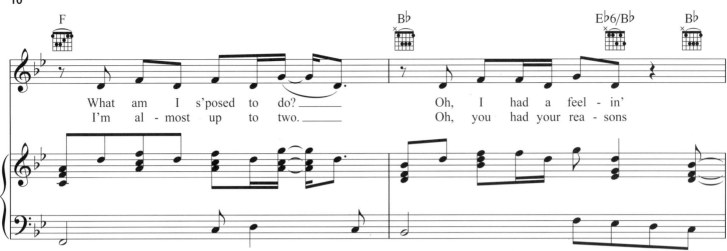

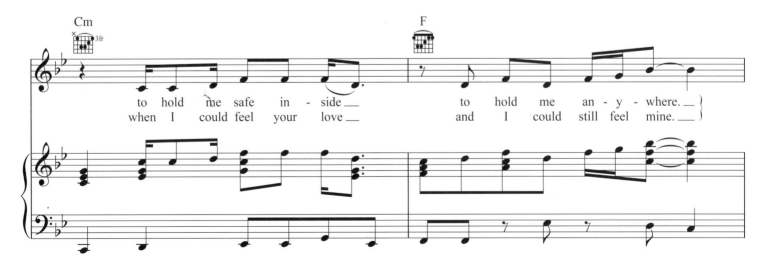

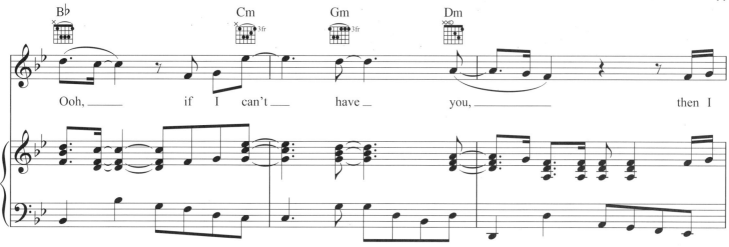

Ooh, _____ if I can't _____ have _____ you, _____ then I

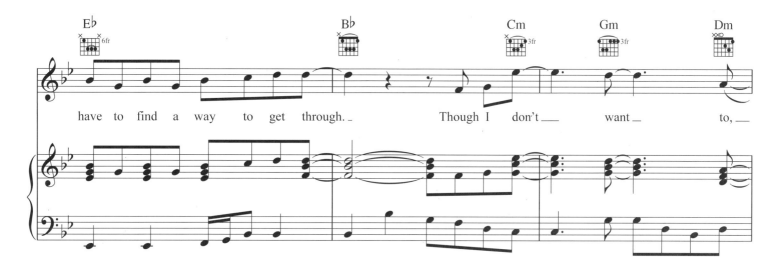

have to find a way to get through. _____ Though I don't _____ want _____ to, _____

I have to do my best to re-call _____ that I'm

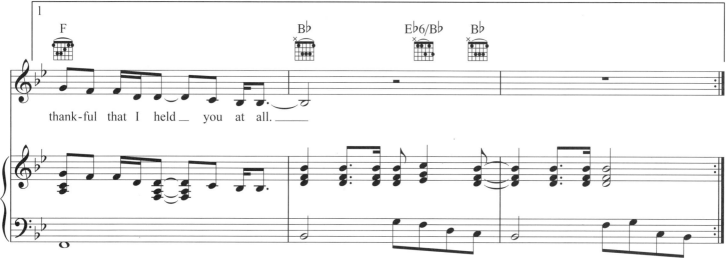

thank-ful that I held _____ you at all. _____

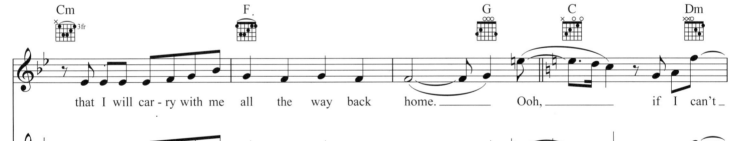

Though I don't ___ want ___ to, _____ I

have to do my best to re - call ___ that I'm thank-ful that I held ___ you at all. ___

Thank - ful that I held you.

(Lead vocal ad lib to end.)

Play 4 times

I'm thank - ful that I held you.

NO SUCH THING

Words and Music by SARA BAREILLES
and JUSTIN TRANTER

Slowly, with a steady beat

I feel you; it's like you're in the next room, at an-y giv-en mo-ment you could re-ap-pear. Thin air, you're out there in it

* *Recorded a half step lower.*

some - where. If I could on - ly get there, _____

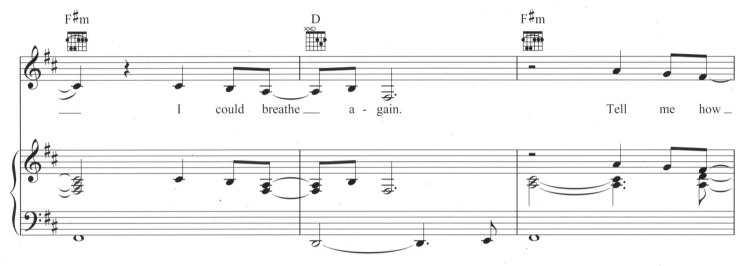

_____ I could breathe _____ a - gain. Tell me how _____

_____ to start. What comes af - ter you? Am I in _____

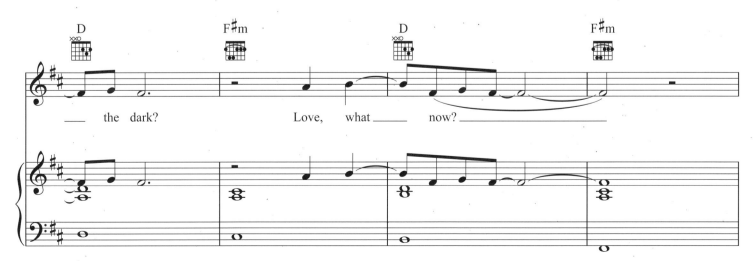

_____ the dark? Love, what _____ now? _____

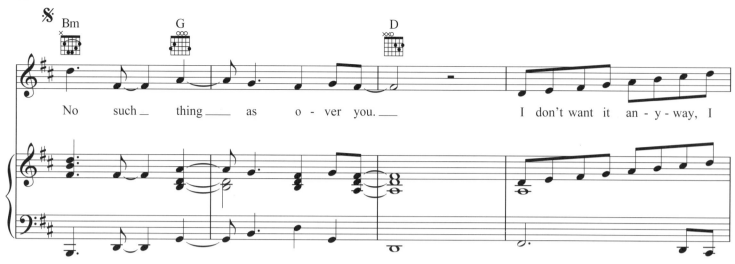

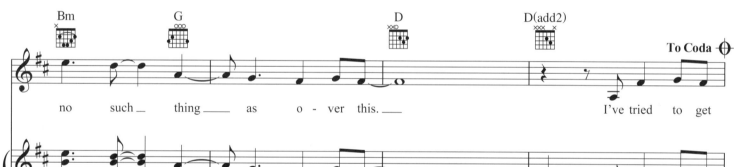

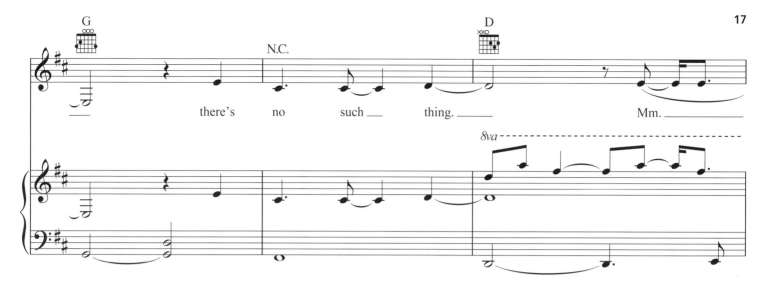

there's no such thing. Mm.

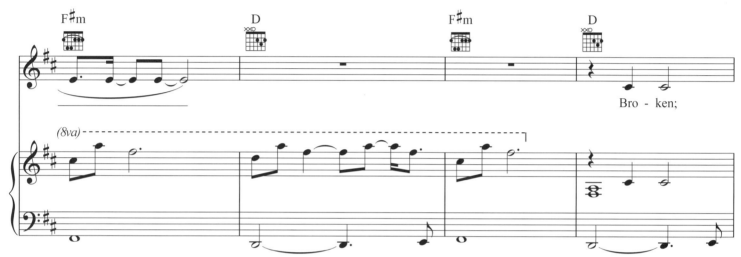

Bro - ken;

you're Rome, I am the ru - ins. The stone I can't

find you in is all that still re - mains.

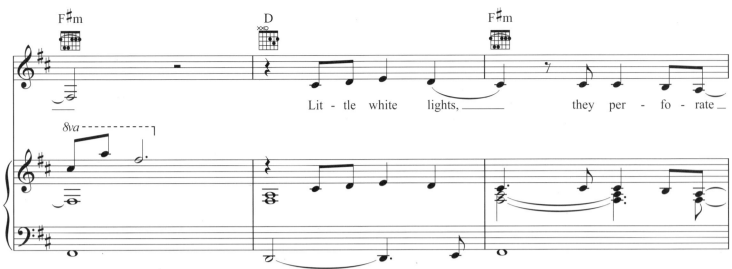

Lit - tle white lights, ____ they per - fo - rate ____

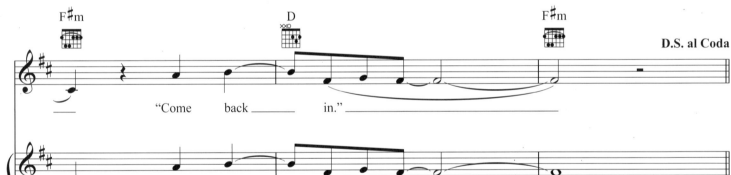

____ ev - 'ry night sky. ____ I say to ____ them ev - 'ry time, ____

D.S. al Coda

"Come back ____ in." ____

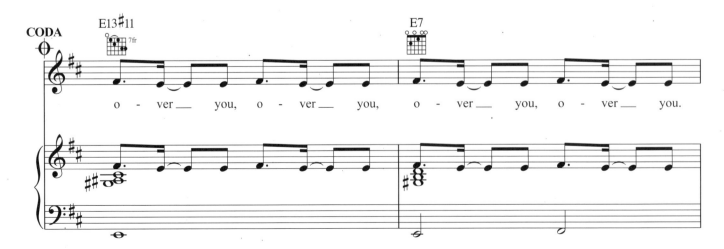

CODA

o - ver ____ you, o - ver ____ you, o - ver ____ you, o - ver ____ you.

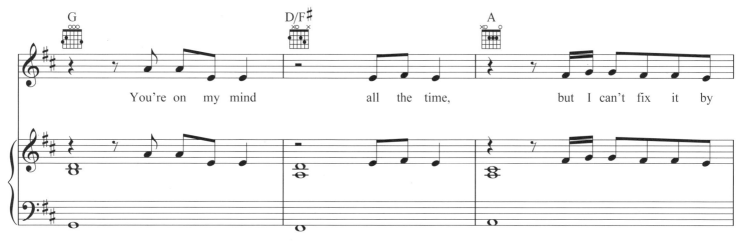

You're on my mind all the time, but I can't fix it by

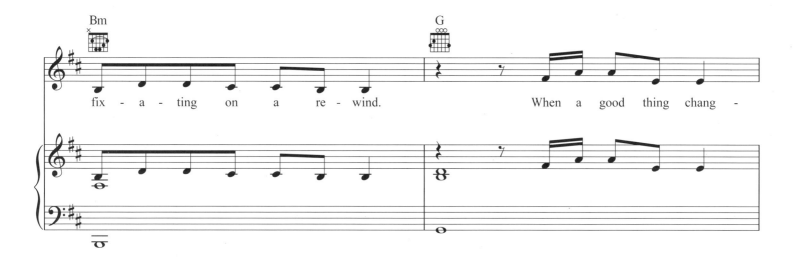

fix - a - ting on a re - wind. When a good thing chang -

es, when the change is stay - ing, ____ on - ly thing to find is what to ____

____ hold on till there's some-thing else ____ to _____ hold on -

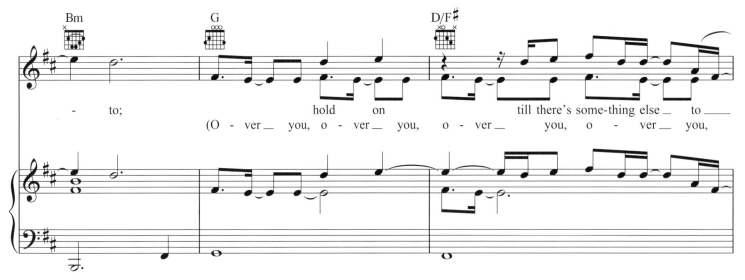

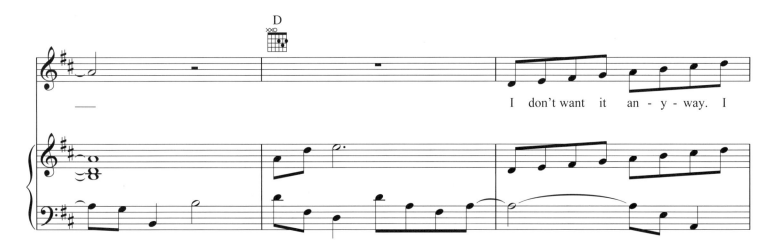

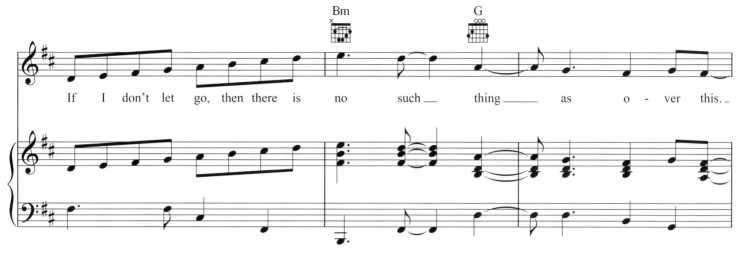

If I don't let go, then there is no such ___ thing ___ as o - ver this. ___

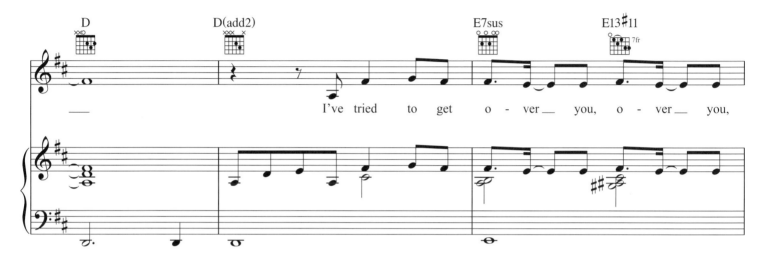

___ I've tried to get o - ver ___ you, o - ver ___ you,

o - ver ___ you, but I ___ think ___ there's no such ___ thing. ___

___ Mm. ___

ARMOR

Words and Music by
SARA BAREILLES
and AARON STERLING

Moderately slow half-time feel

Let it be-gin; let Ad-am in. Step one: O-rig-i-nal Sin. Un-der-neath the leaves, Ad-am found Eve.

Both of them found some-thing sweet un-der the ap-ple tree. Then it ___ was o-

* Recorded a half step lower.

ver; roads _ di - vide. _____ Step two: learn-ing how to lie.

Let me as a ques - tion to pres-ent day: _ How the hell did Eve _ end up

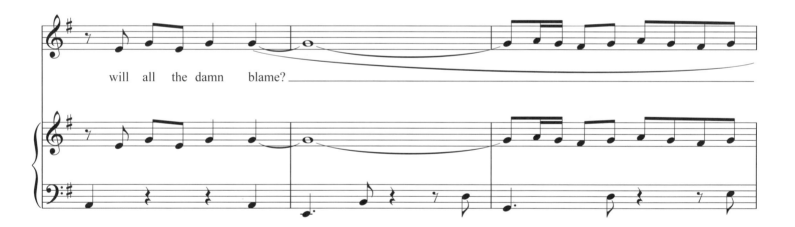

will all the damn blame? _____

All the damn blame. _____

To _____ all the dirt-y looks, the kit-ty cat calls, ___

___ to the ones who try and throw us up a-gainst the back walls, let me tell you some-

-thing you'll un-der-stand: On-ly the lit-tle boys ___ tell you they're a big man.

To all ___ my ___ sis-ters and all our ___ friends, ___ we have to

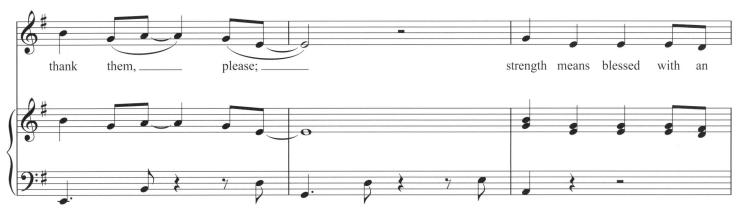

thank them, _____ please; _____ strength means blessed with an

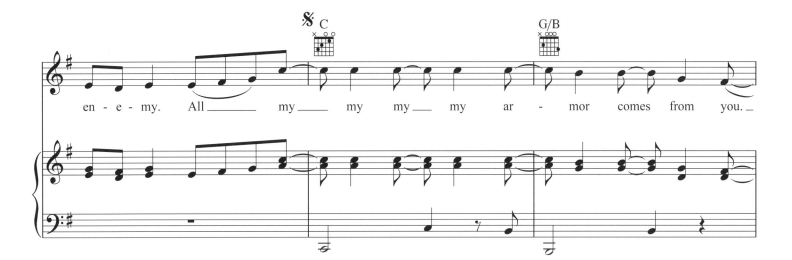

en-e-my. All _____ my _____ my my _____ my ar-mor comes from you. _____

_____ You make me try, _____ try, try, _____ try hard-

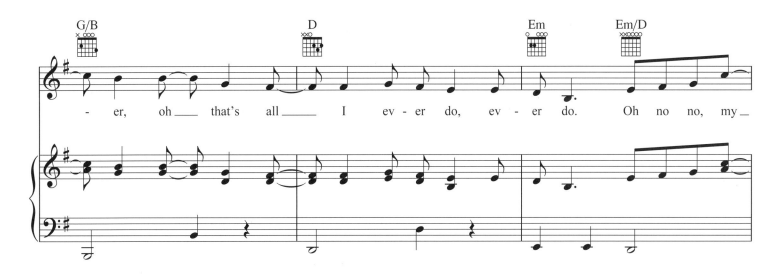

-er, oh _____ that's all _____ I ev-er do, ev-er do. Oh no no, my _____

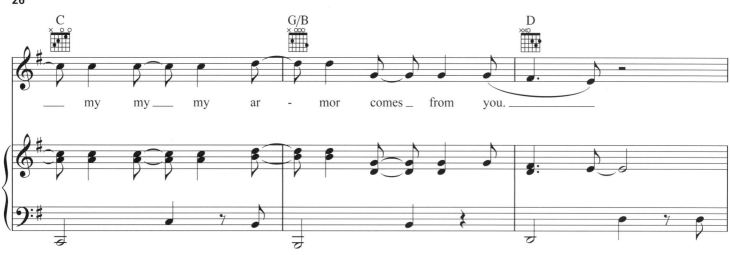

my my my ar - mor comes from you.

You make me strong - er, strong - er.

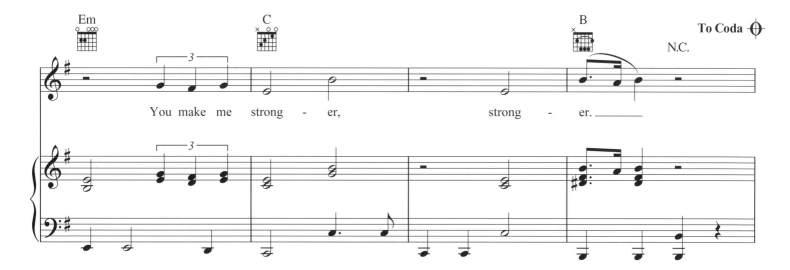

Hand me my ar - mor.

(Hand me my ar - mor. Hand

_____ me my ar - mor.) Step _____ three: I see _____ the un - for -

get - ta - ble in - cred - i - ble ones _____ who came be - fore me;

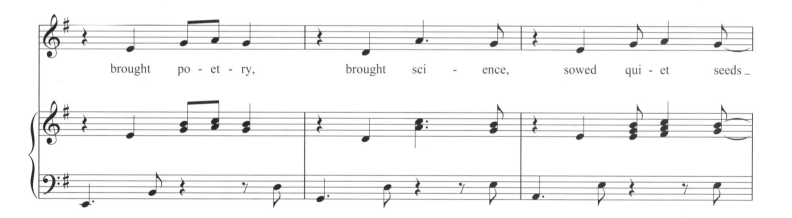

brought po - et - ry, brought sci - ence, sowed qui - et seeds _____

_____ of self - re - li - ance; bloomed _ in _____ me, _____ so _____

_____ here I ___ am. _____ You think I _____ am high ___ and might-y, mis-

D.S. al Coda

-ter? Wait till you meet my lit-tle sis - ter. All _____ my _

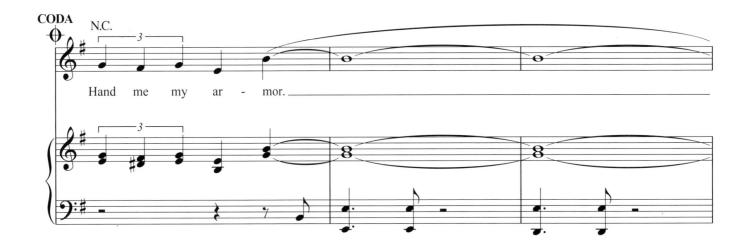

CODA N.C.

Hand me my ar - mor. _____

____ men on - ly set the world on fire. _____ Sad ___ you can't

see it. You ___ brought the flame, here ___ comes the phoe - nix. ___

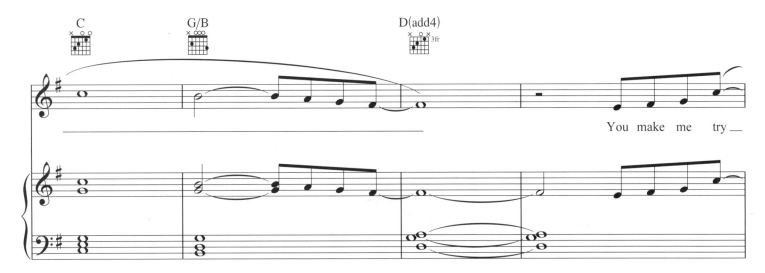

C G/B D(add4)

_____ You make me try___

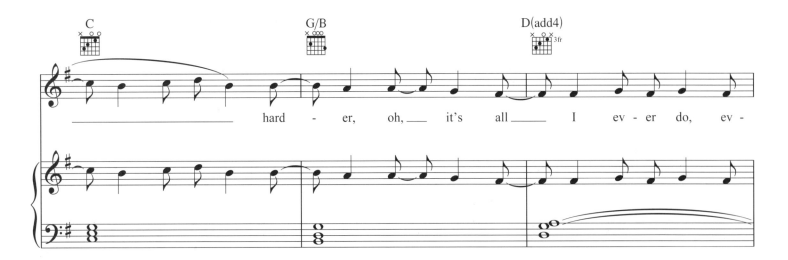

C G/B D(add4)

_____ hard - er, oh, it's all ____ I ev - er do, ev -

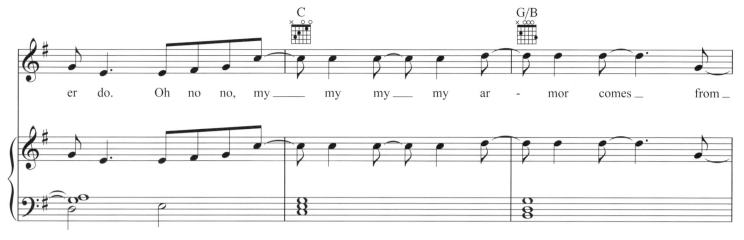

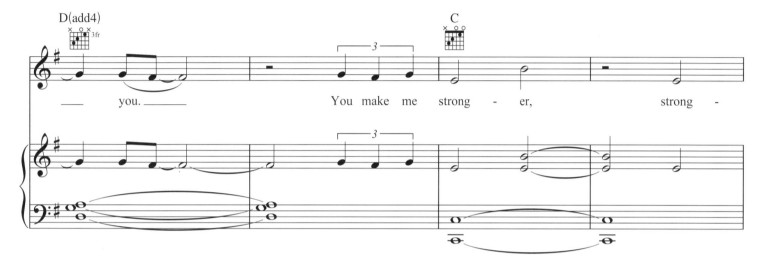

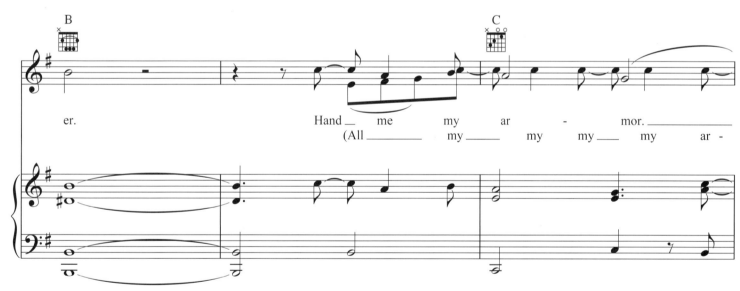

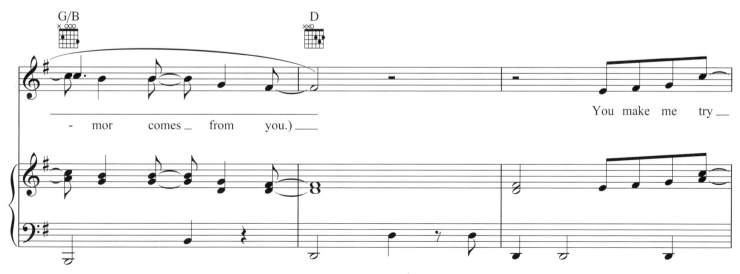

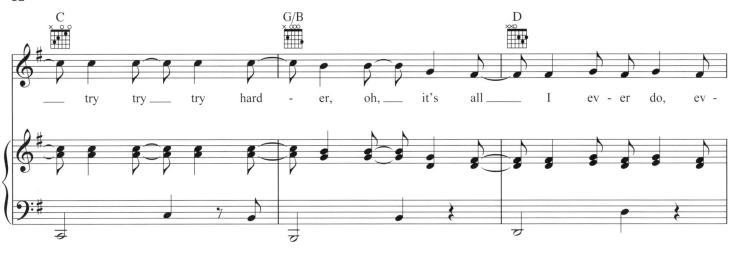

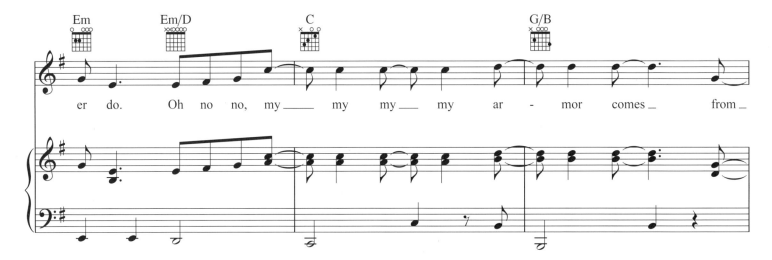

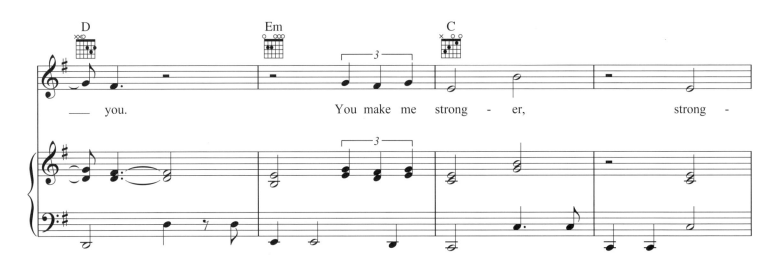

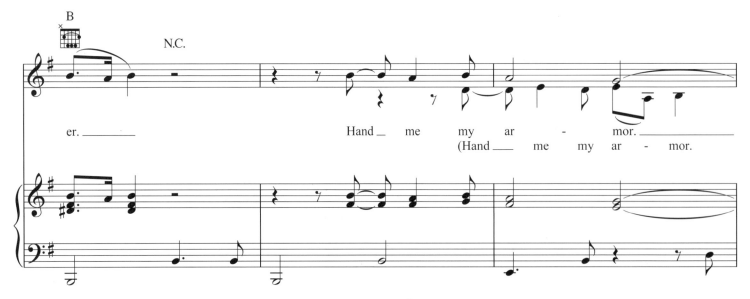

Hand ___ me my ar - mor. Hand _

___ me my ar - mor. Hand ___ me my ar - mor.) ___

Hand ___ me my ar - mor. Hand _

___ me my ar - mor. Hand ___ me my ar - mor.

EYES ON YOU

Words and Music by
SARA BAREILLES

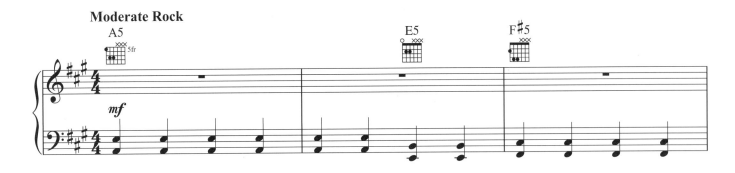

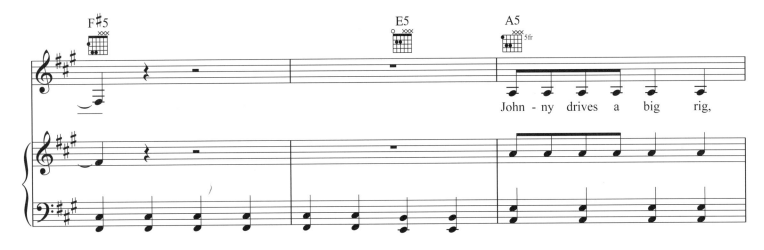

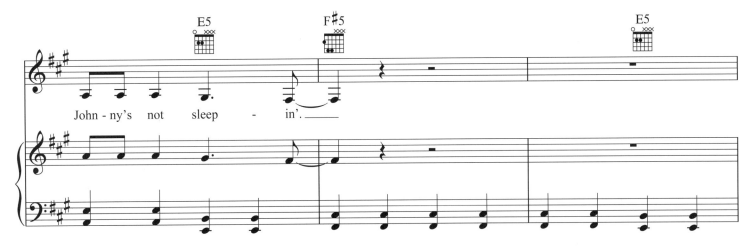

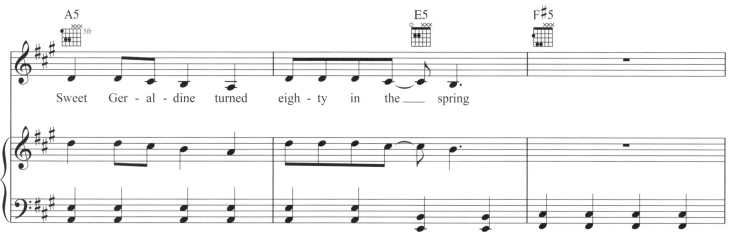

Sweet Ger - al - dine turned eigh - ty in the ___ spring

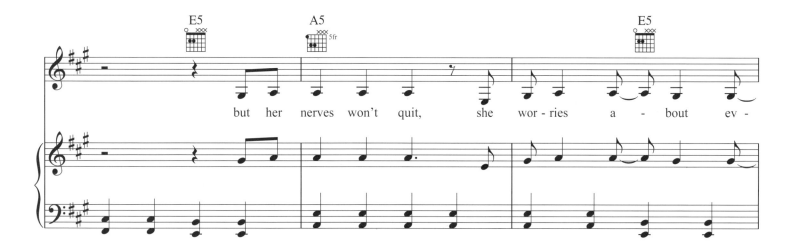

but her nerves won't quit, she wor - ries a - bout ev -

- 'ry - thing. ___

Sar - ah's on a work trip,
Tom - my took a free fall,

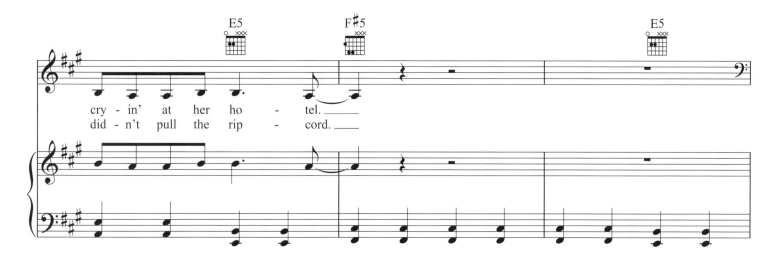

cry - in' at her ho - tel. ___
did - n't pull the rip - cord. ___

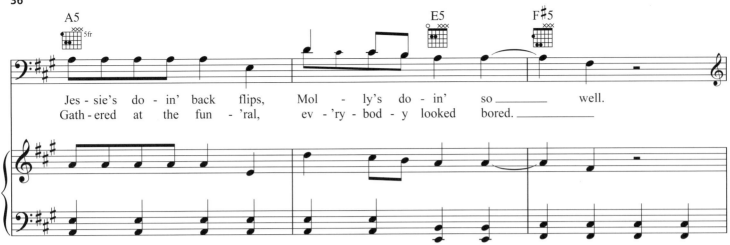

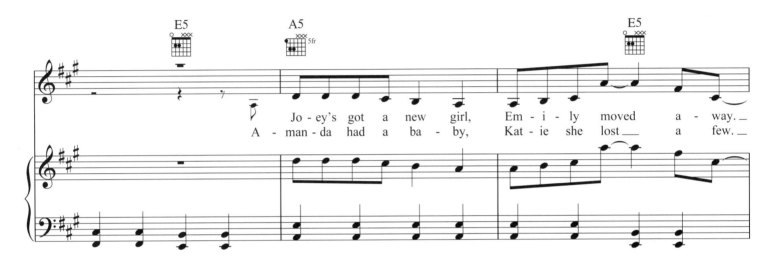

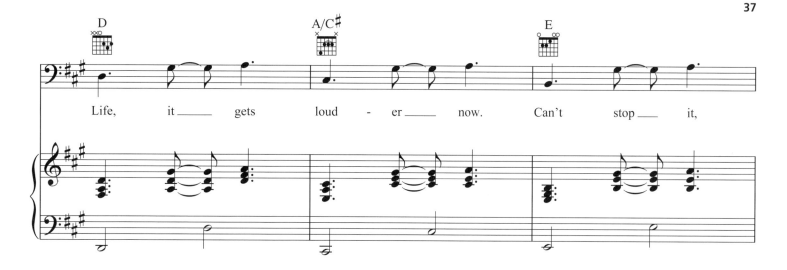

Life, it ___ gets loud - er ___ now. Can't stop ___ it,

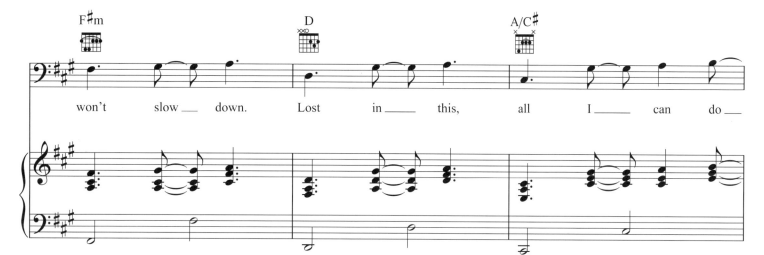

won't slow ___ down. Lost in ___ this, all I ___ can do ___

___ is keep my eyes ___ on you. I know the world ___

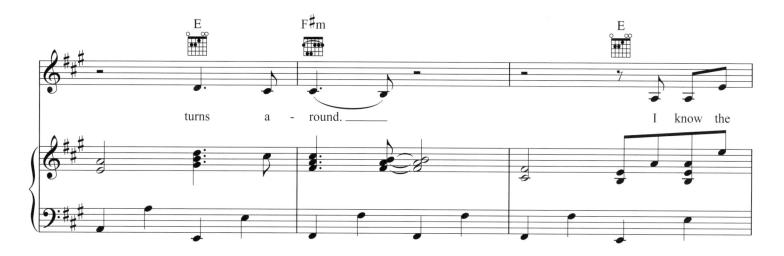

turns a - round. ___ I know the

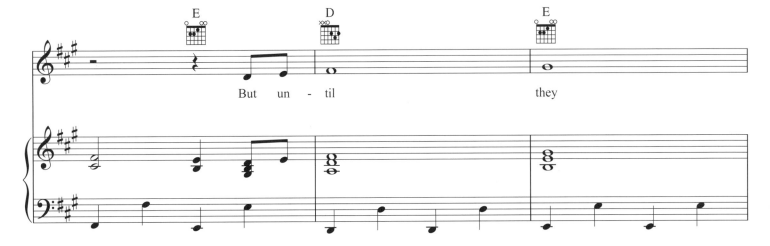

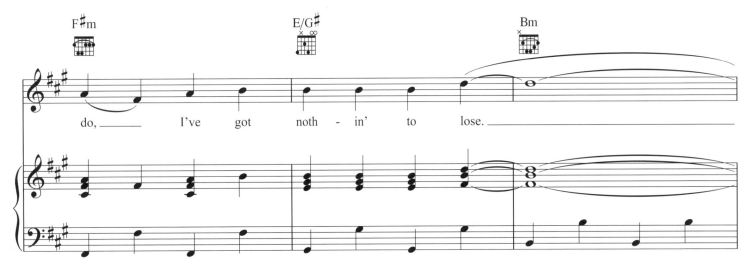

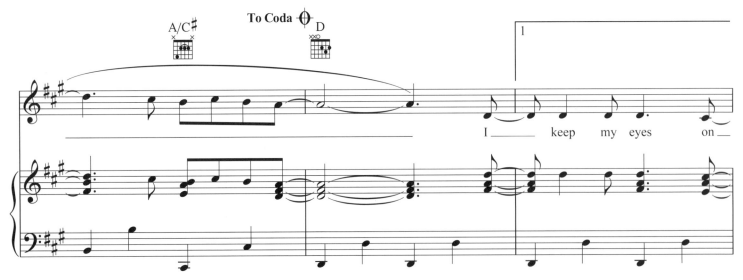

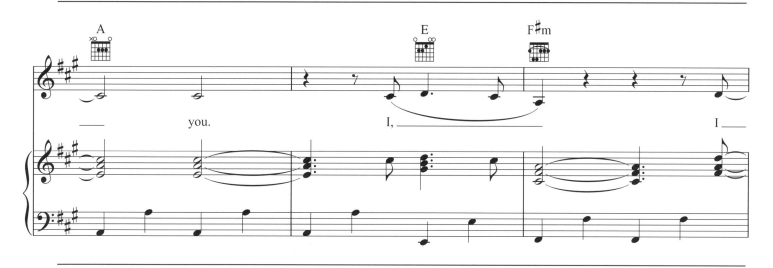

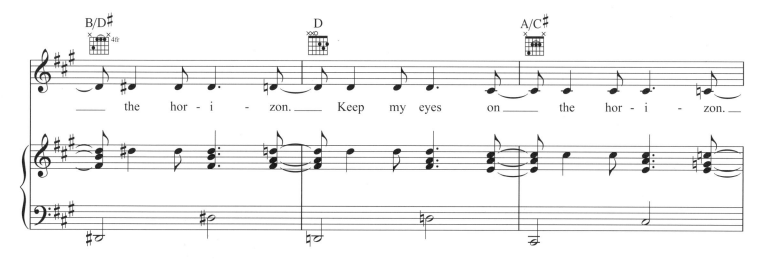

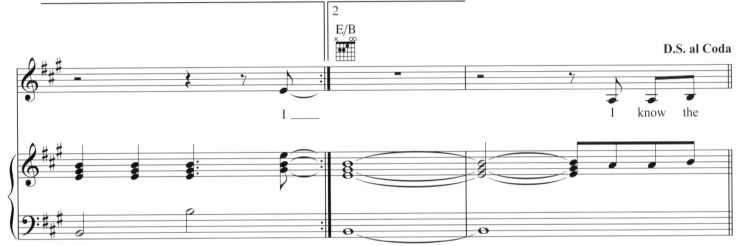

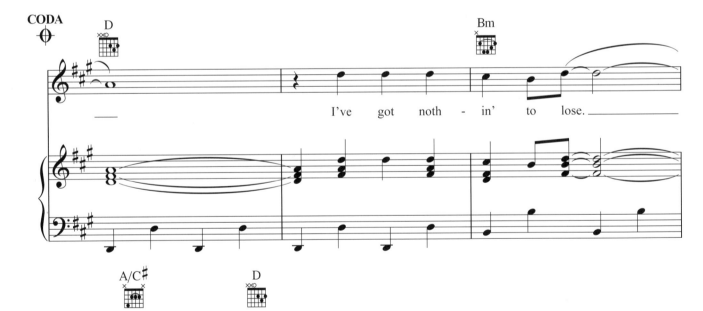

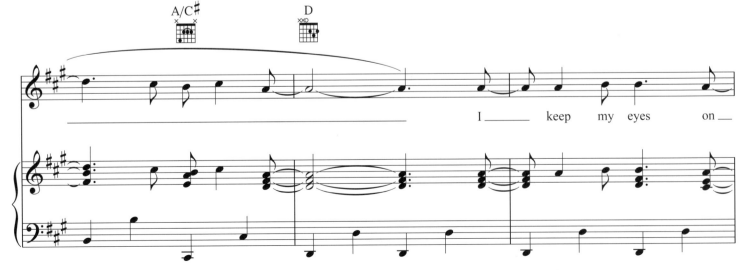

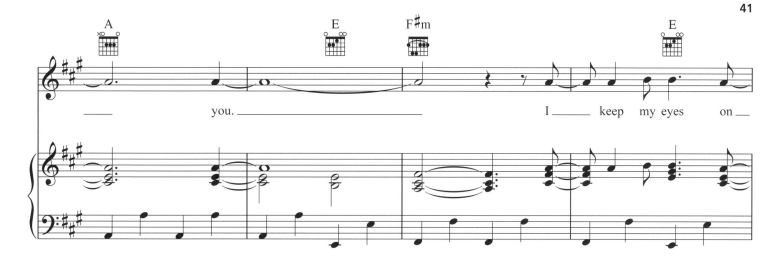

you. _____ I _____ keep my eyes on ____

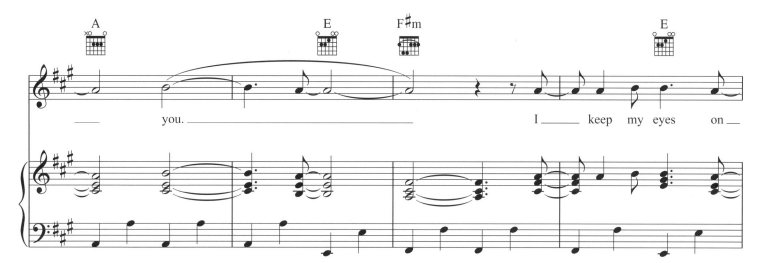

you. _____ I _____ keep my eyes on ____

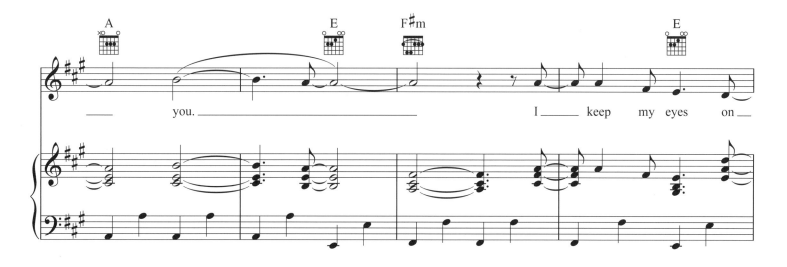

you. _____ I _____ keep my eyes on ____

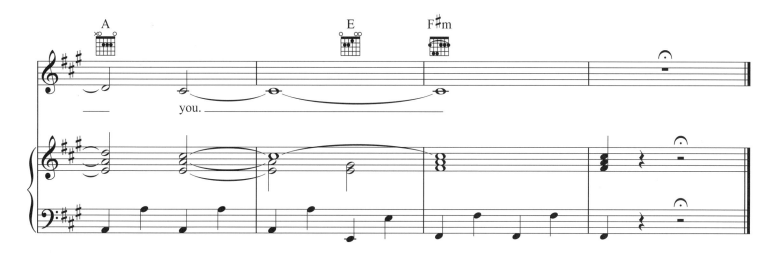

you. _____

MISS SIMONE

Words and Music by SARA BAREILLES
and LORI McKENNA

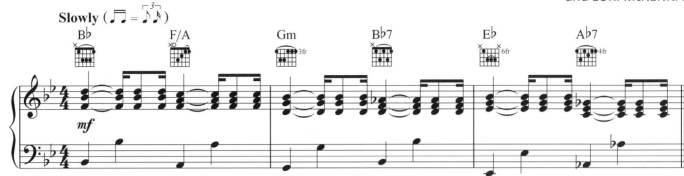

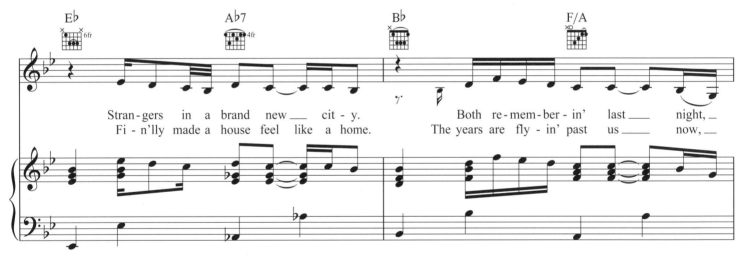

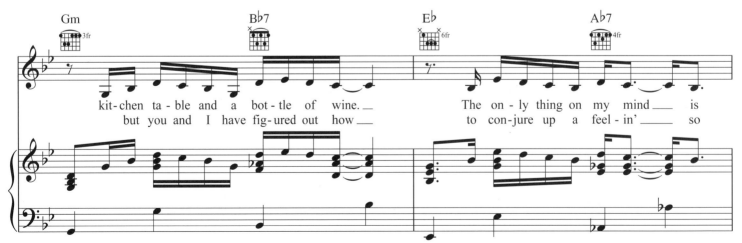

Smiles __ in the morn-in' at __ me, a-part-ment on the sec-ond sto-ry.
Mov-in' box-es cov-er the __ floor. I've nev-er quite been here be-fore. __

Stran-gers in a brand new __ cit-y. Both re-mem-ber-in' last __ night, __
Fi-n'lly made a house feel like a home. The years are fly-in' past us __ now, __

kit-chen ta-ble and a bot-tle of wine. __ The on-ly thing on my mind __ is
but you and I have fig-ured out how __ to con-jure up a feel-in' __ so

you. _____
true. _____

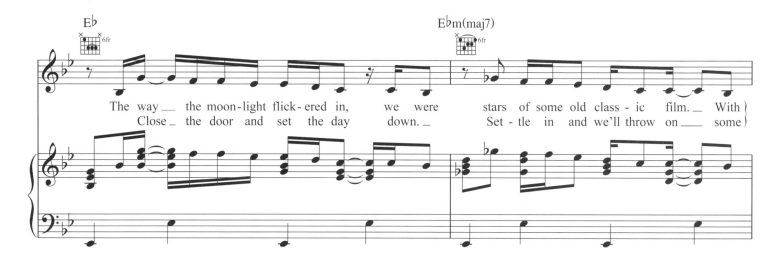

The way __ the moon-light flick-ered in, we were stars of some old clas-ic film. __ With
Close __ the door and set the day down. __ Set-tle in and we'll throw on __ some

Miss Si-mone __ sing-in', "Pour some __ su-gar in __ my bowl, __ ba-by."

In the glow __ of the can - dle-light, __ we __ danced __ all __ night.
In the glow __ of the can - dle-light __ we can dance __ all __ night.
In the glow __ of the can - dle-light __ we will dance __ all __ night.

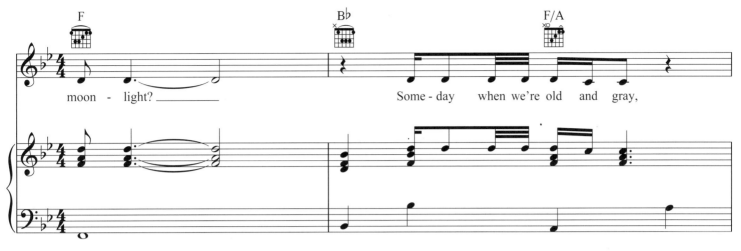

moon - light? _____ Some - day when we're old and gray,

sift - in' through our ___ yes - ter- days, we'll ___ pull that mem -'ry from it's sleeve ___ and

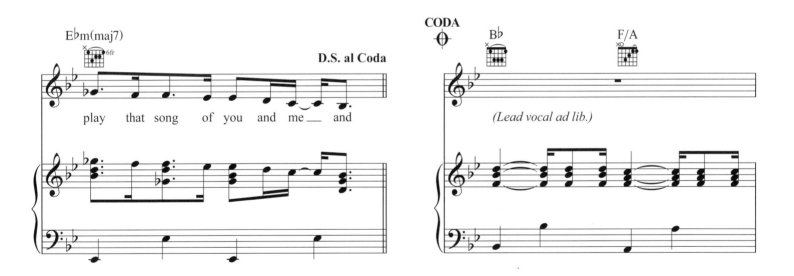

play that song of you and me ___ and

D.S. al Coda

CODA

(Lead vocal ad lib.)

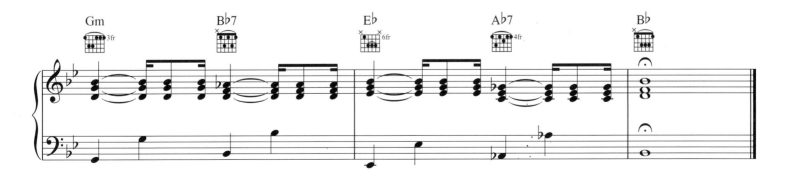

WICKED LOVE

Words and Music by
SARA BAREILLES

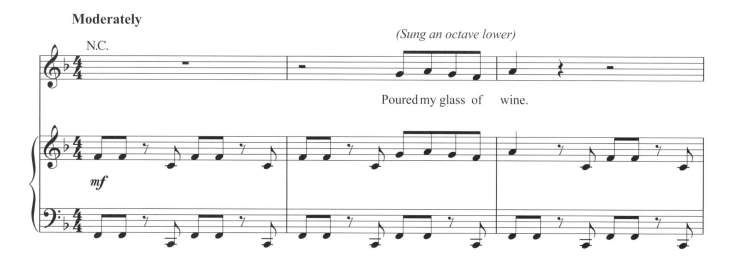

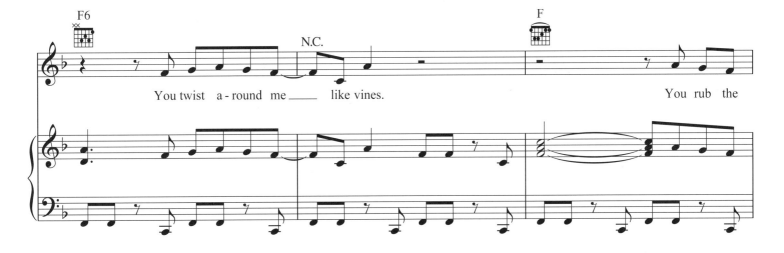

You twist a - round me _____ like vines. You rub the

stars in my bright eyes. Then you sold me a fu - ture from the

(Sung as written)

ones you had in the trunk of your car. You said I

think too much.
think too much.

You said I al - ways mess it up. _____
Tell me I al - ways mess it up. _____

It was so eas-y to be-lieve. I've al-ways said the same things. __
Well, I'll break the glass and see if the fire - flies a-gree. __

Stay out, hon-ey. I __ can see __ you're wick-ed. __

I __ don't want your wick-ed love. __ Don't need what makes __

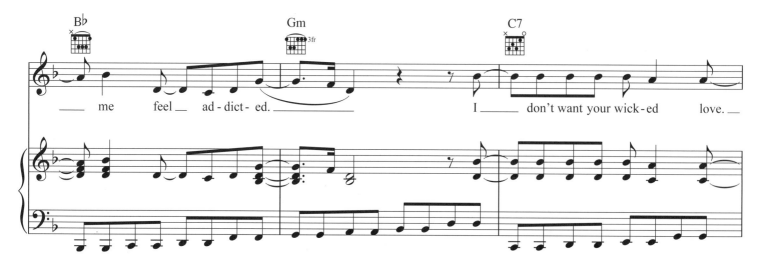

__ me feel __ ad-dict-ed. __ I __ don't want your wick-ed love. __

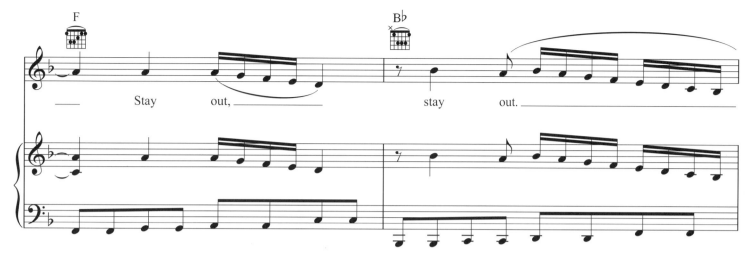

Stay out, _____ stay out. _____

I _____ don't want your wick-ed love. _____ Stay out, _____

stay out. _____ I _____

To Coda ⊕

_____ don't want your wick-ed, wick-ed, wick-ed love. _____

How her ham-mer and nails __ chis-el beau-ty from gro-tesque things. __

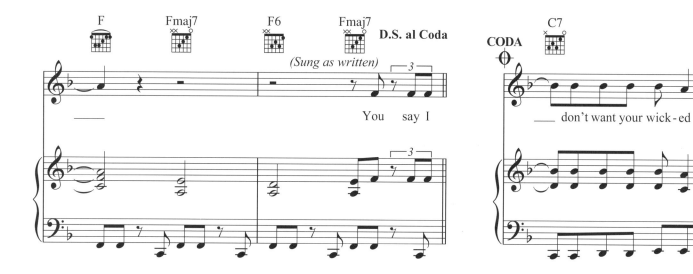

D.S. al Coda

(Sung as written)

You say I

CODA

__ don't want your wick-ed love. __

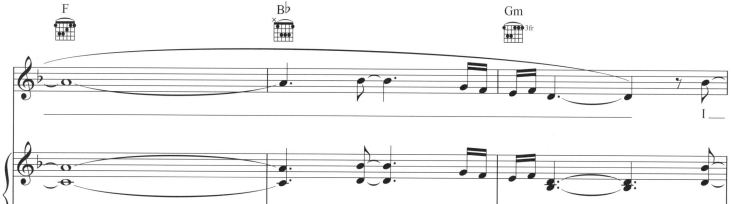

I __

__ don't want your wick-ed love. __ Don't need what makes __ me feel __ ad-dict-ed. __

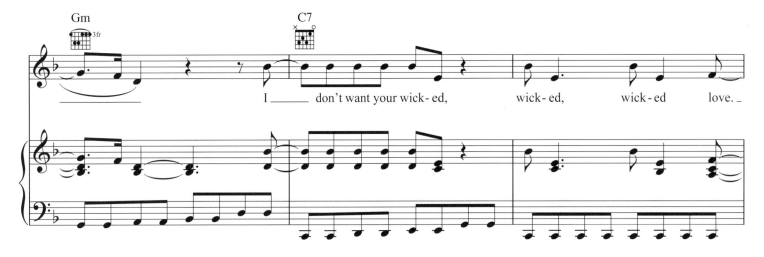

SAINT HONESTY

Words and Music by SARA BAREILLES
and LORI McKENNA

Slow Gospel feel

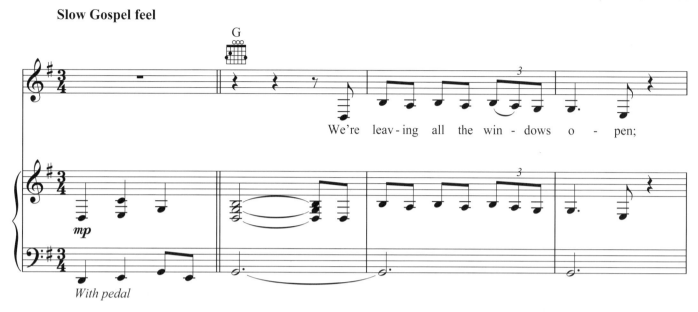

We're leav-ing all the win-dows o-pen;

we don't e-ven mind _____ the rain,

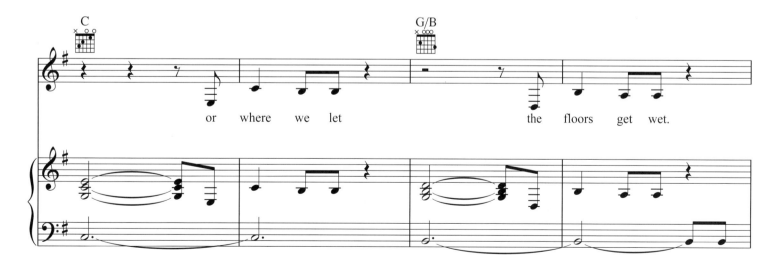

or where we let the floors get wet.

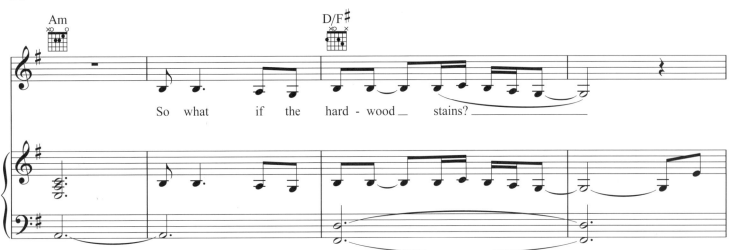

So what if the hard-wood __ stains? _____

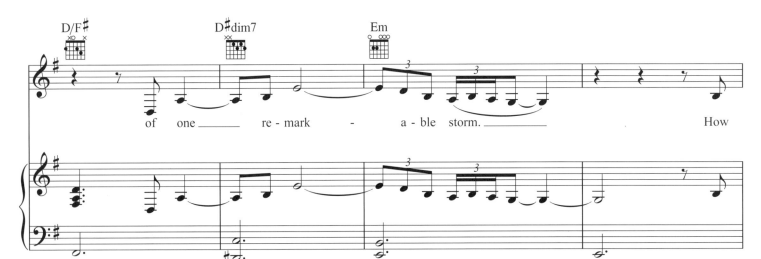

'Cause we're col-lect-ing ev - i - dence

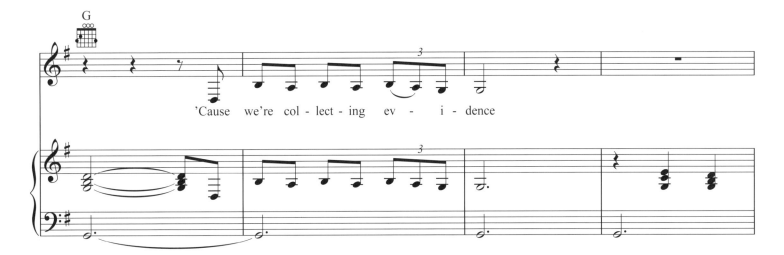

of one __ re-mark - a-ble storm. _____ How

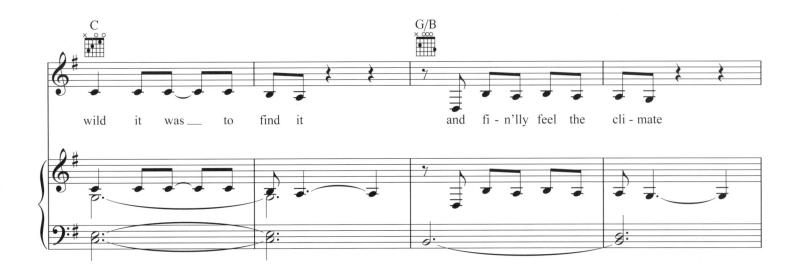

wild it was __ to find it and fi-n'lly feel the cli-mate

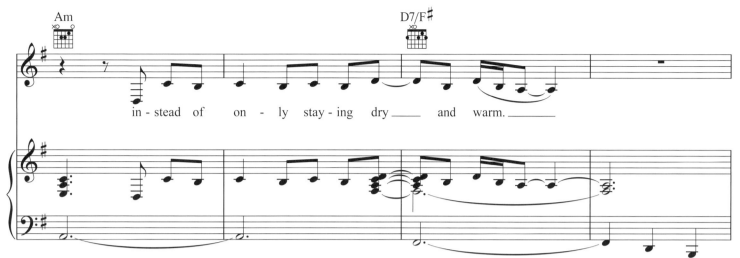

in - stead of on - ly stay-ing dry ____ and warm. ____

Rain _____ on ____ us, ____ Saint _____

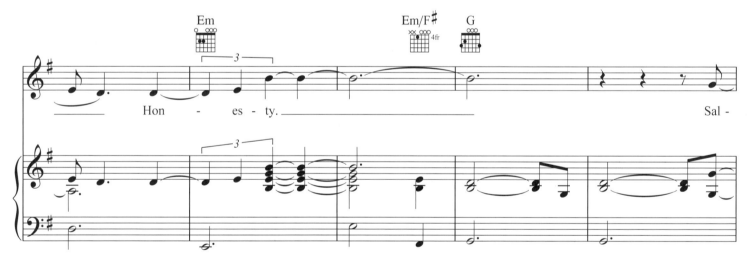

____ Hon - es - ty. _____ Sal -

- va - tion ____ is com - ing in the morn - ing, { but } { and }

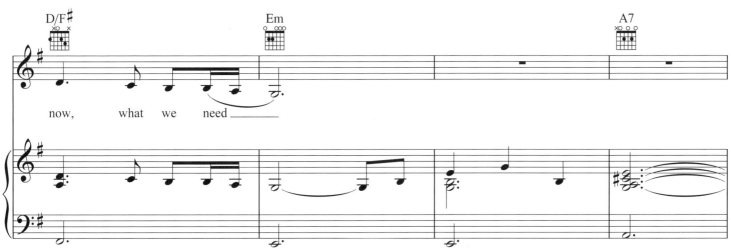

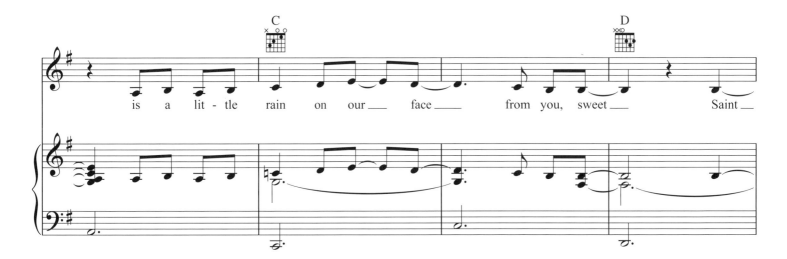

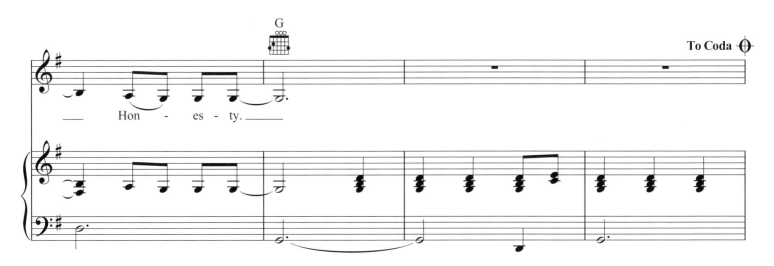

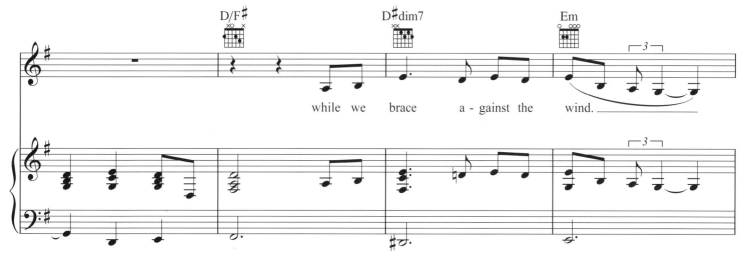

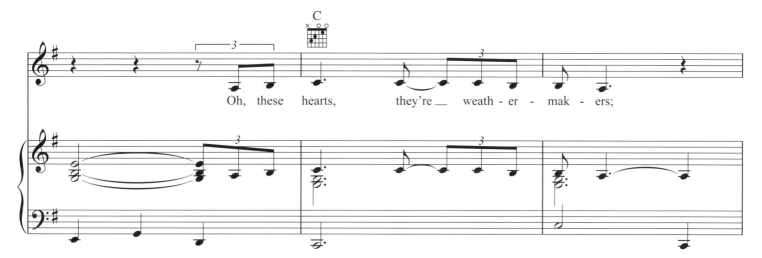

while we brace a - gainst the wind. ____

Oh, these hearts, they're ___ weath - er - mak - ers;

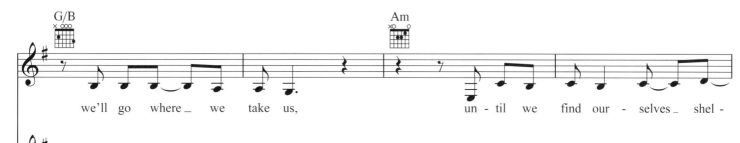

we'll go where ___ we take us, un - til we find our - selves ___ shel -

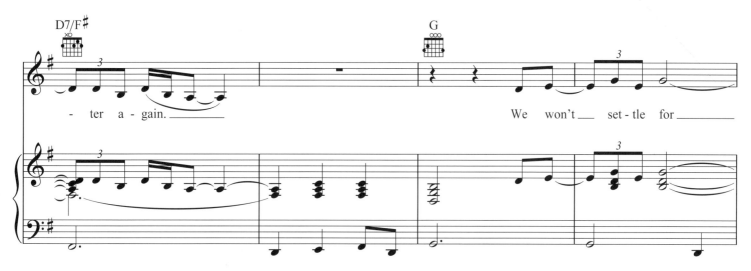

- ter a - gain. ____   We won't ___ set - tle for ____

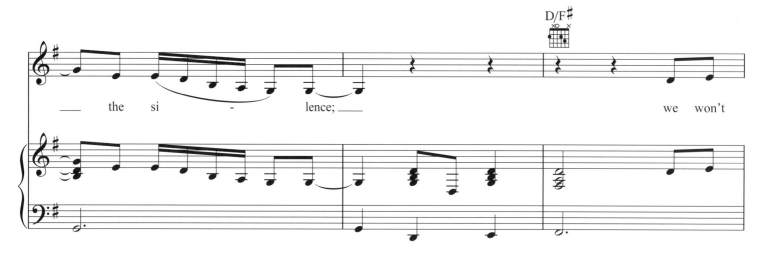

the si - lence; ___ we won't

drown ___ in the tears. ___ We'll say ev - 'ry sin - gle

word, ___ e - ven if we think ___ they'll hurt; let the

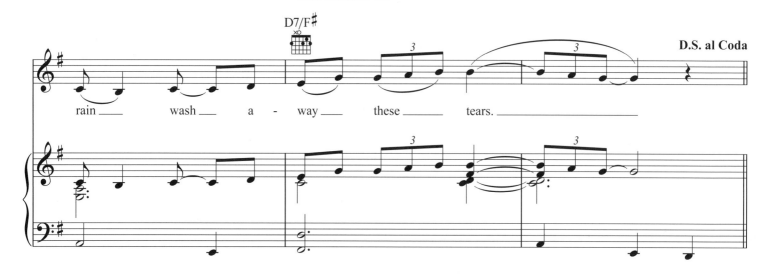

rain ___ wash ___ a - way ___ these ___ tears. ___

Oh, _____ we won't let go; _____ we'll __ be

soaked _____ to the bone. ___ Bap - tized by truth, we will

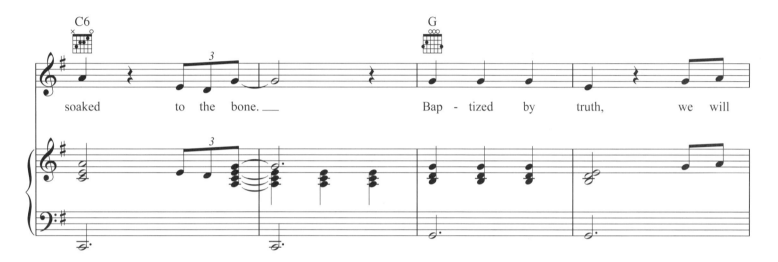

reap what we ___ sow, _____ build our own high - er ground _

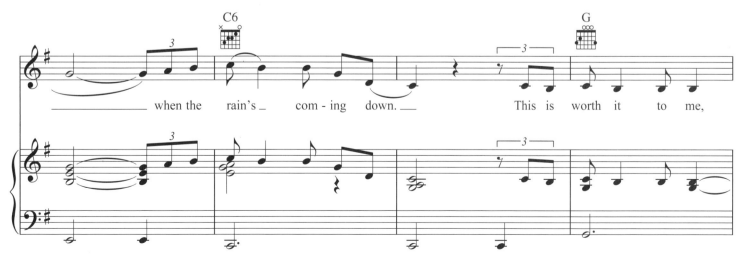

_____ when the rain's _ com - ing down. ___ This is worth it to me,

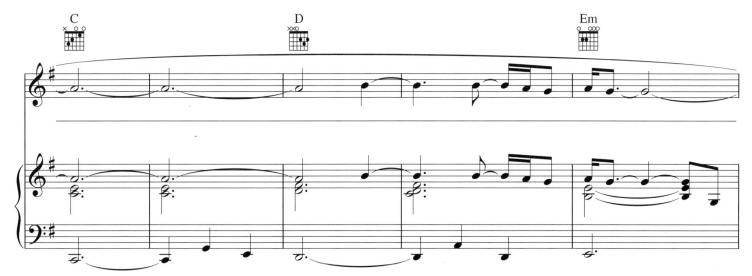

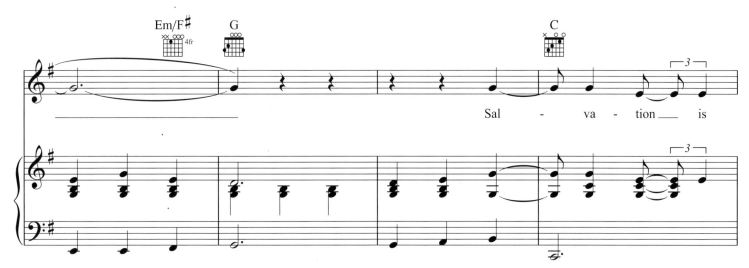

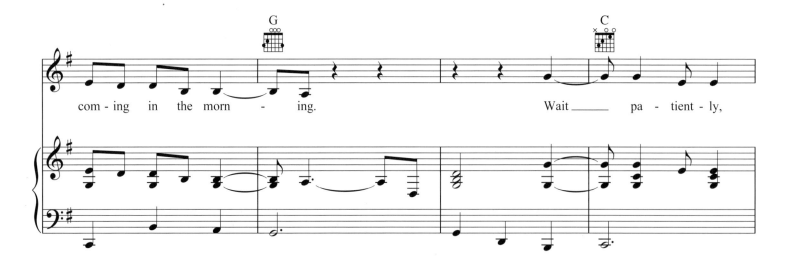

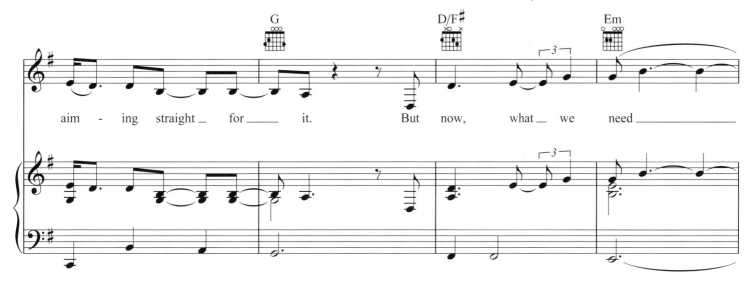

aim - ing straight _ for _ it. But now, what _ we need _____

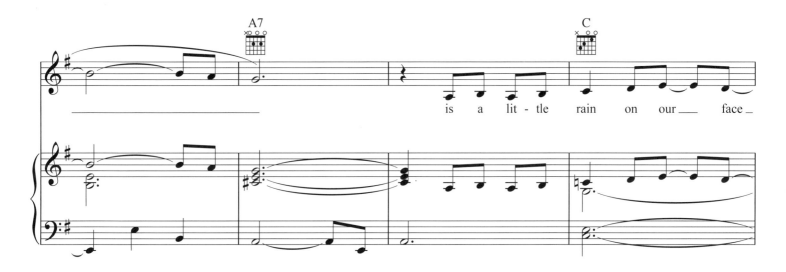

_____ is a lit - tle rain on our _ face _

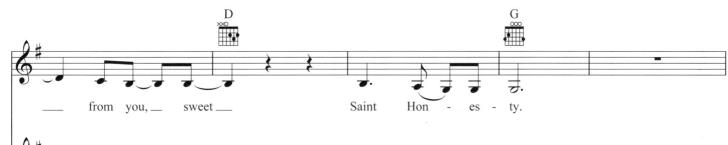

_ from you, _ sweet _ Saint Hon - es - ty.

ORPHEUS

Words and Music by
SARA BAREILLES

Come by the fire. Lay __ down your head. My __ love, I see you're grow-ing tired, so set the bad day __ by the bed __ and rest a-

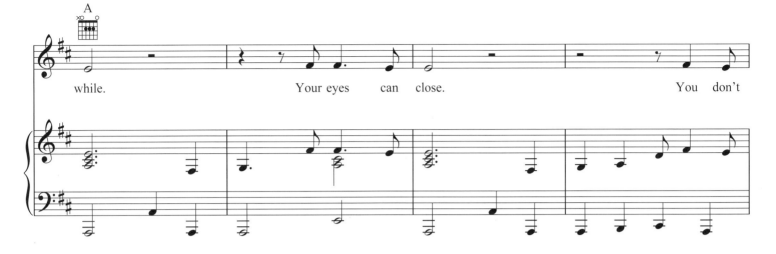

while. Your eyes can close. You don't

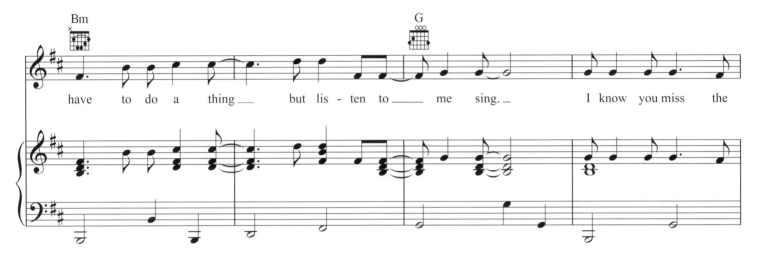

have to do a thing ___ but lis-ten to ___ me sing. ___ I know you miss the

world. The one you knew. The one where

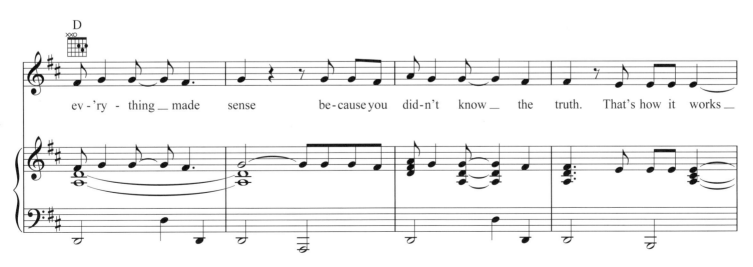

ev-'ry-thing ___ made sense be-cause you did-n't know ___ the truth. That's how it works ___

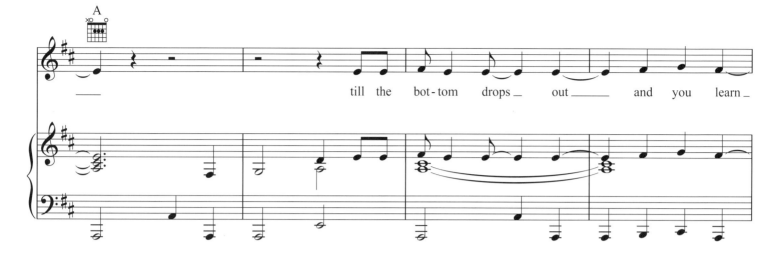

till the bot-tom drops _ out _ and you learn _

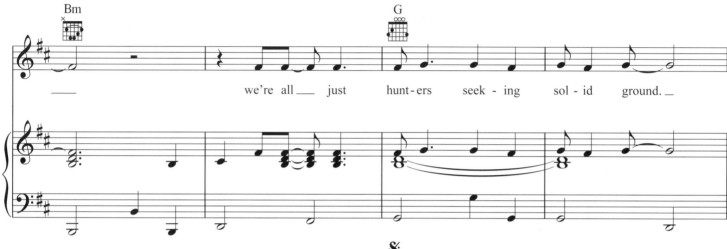

we're all _ just hunt-ers seek - ing sol - id ground. _

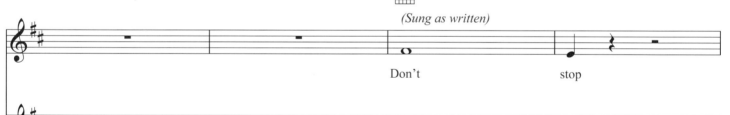

(Sung as written)

Don't stop

try'n' to find me here a-midst the cha - os. _____

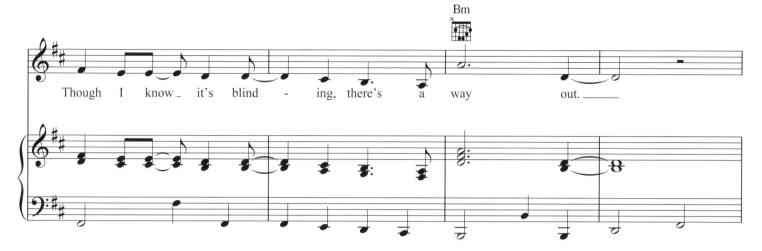

Though I know __ it's blind - ing, there's __ a way __ out. ___

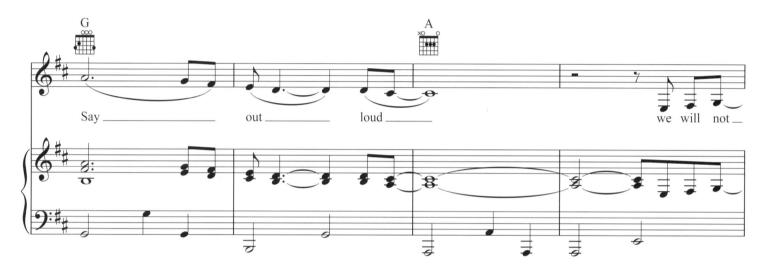

Say _____ out _____ loud _____ we will not __

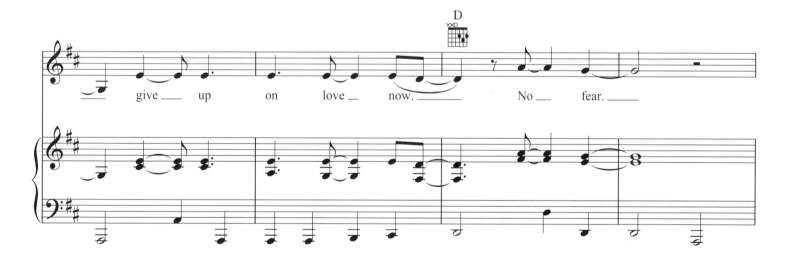

give __ up on love __ now. ___ No __ fear. ___

Don't you turn like Or - phe - us, ___ just __ stay here. ___

Hold me in the dark _____ and when _____ the day _____ ap - pears, _____

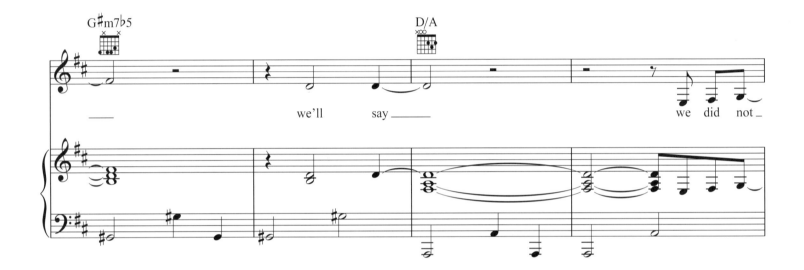

_____ we'll say _____ we did not _____

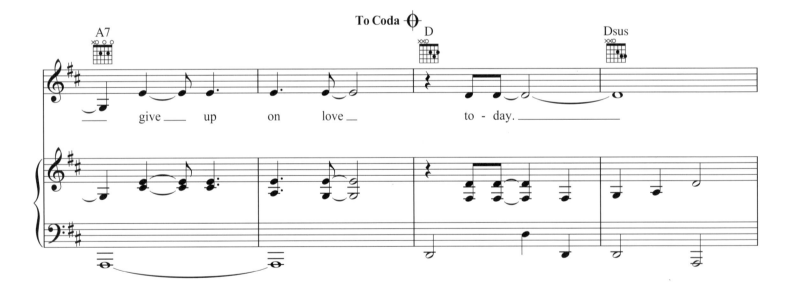

give _____ up on love _____ to - day. _____

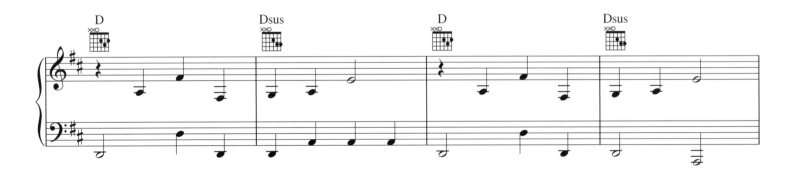

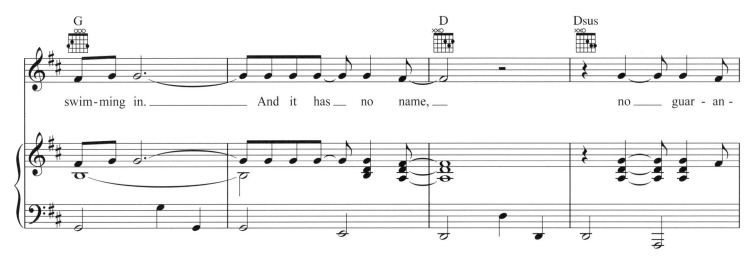

swim-ming in. _____ And it has __ no name, _____ no ___ guar-an-

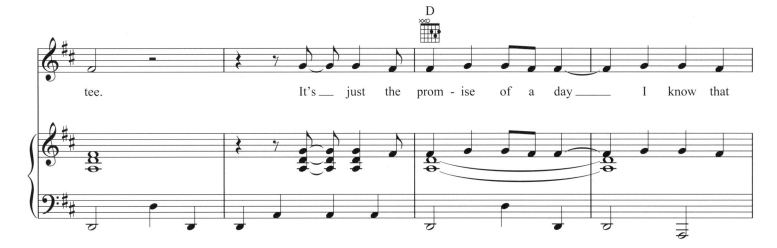

tee. It's __ just the prom-ise of a day _____ I know that

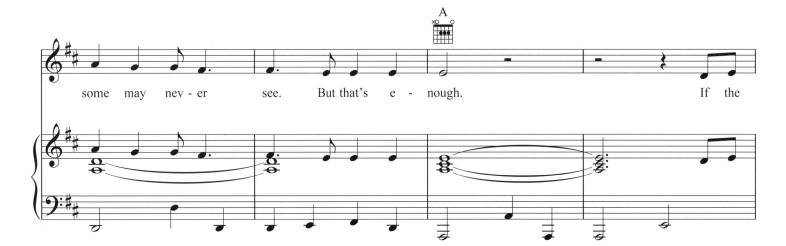

some may nev-er see. But that's e - nough. If the

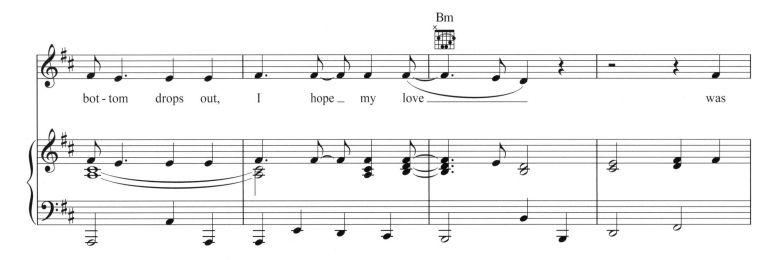

bot-tom drops out, I hope __ my love _____ was

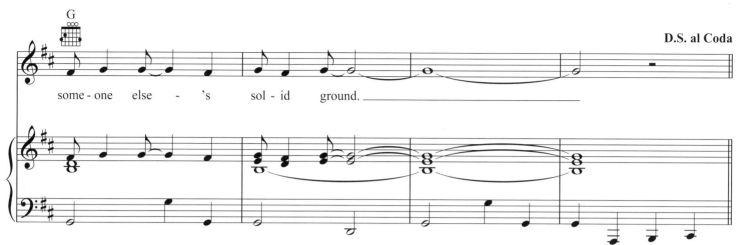

D.S. al Coda

some-one else - 's sol - id ground.

CODA

to - day.   We'll say

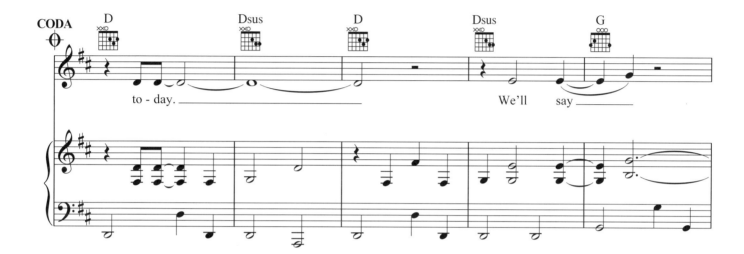

we did not ___ give ___ up   on   love ___   to - day. ___

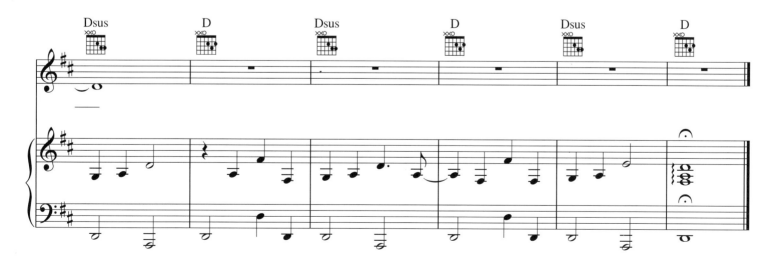

POETRY BY DEAD MEN

Words and Music by SARA BAREILLES
and JUSTIN TRANTER

you can turn a-round, ___ one last look ___ at the girl ___ you lost ___ in the time ___ you ___

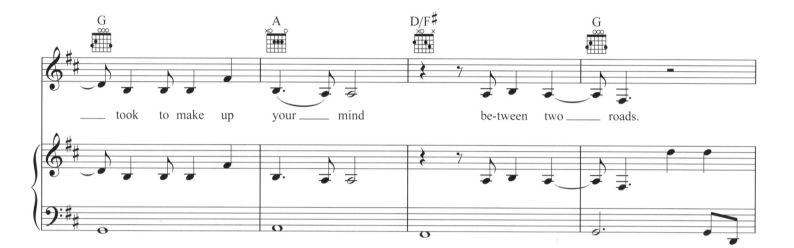

___ took to make up your ___ mind be-tween two ___ roads.

Go and take some more time, but ___ me and mine must go.

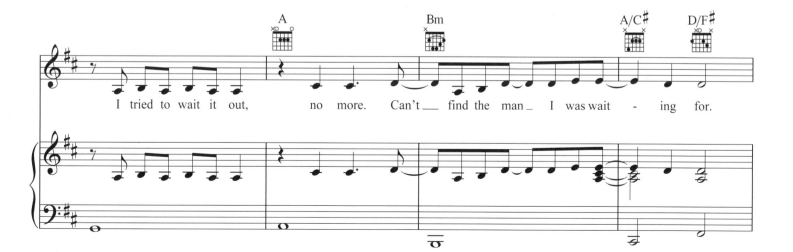

I tried to wait it out, no more. Can't ___ find the man ___ I was wait - ing for.

I want-ed to be your girl in a white T - shirt ____ o - ver cof - fee,

stir-ring in ____ the cin - na - mon while you read me po - et - ry by dead men.

I want-ed to be your girl with your hands on ____ my ____ skin,

stir-ring in ____ the cin - na - mon while you read me po - et - ry by

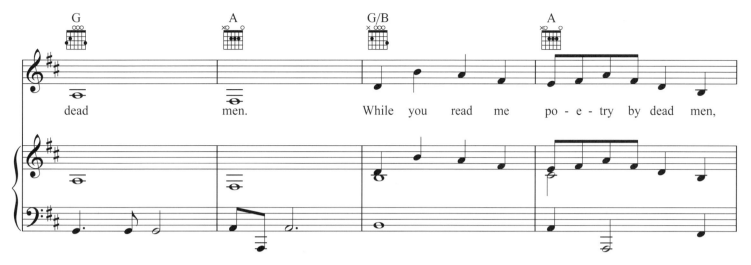

dead men. While you read me po-e-try by dead men,

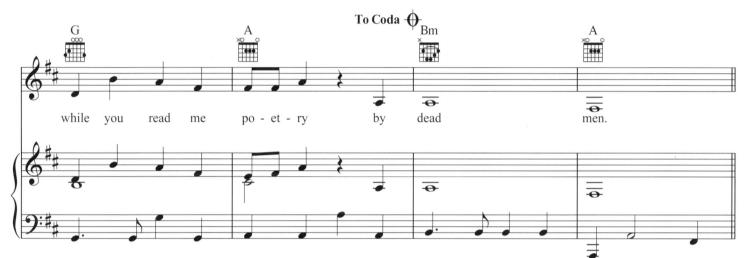

To Coda ⊕

while you read me po-et-ry by dead men.

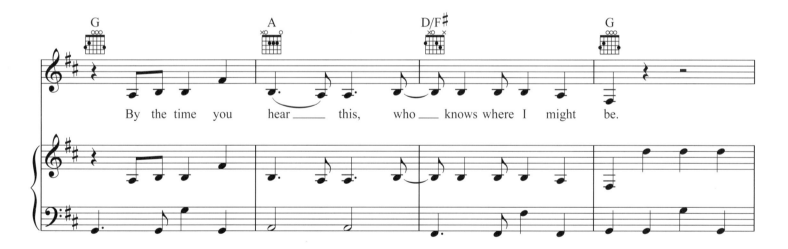

By the time you hear _____ this, who _____ knows where I might be.

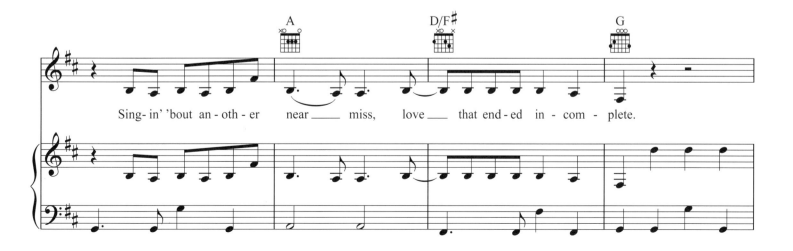

Sing-in' 'bout an-oth-er near _____ miss, love _____ that end-ed in-com-plete.

I was read-y, but ___ you weren't, so jump ___ with your net ___ from this bridge ___ you've burned.

I want-ed to tell ___ you things, all the se-crets I've ___ been keep-ing.

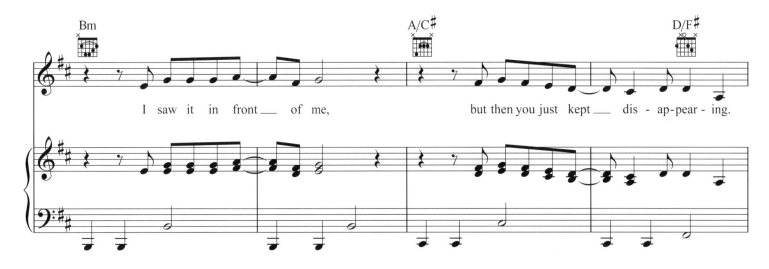

I saw it in front ___ of me, but then you just kept ___ dis-ap-pear-ing.

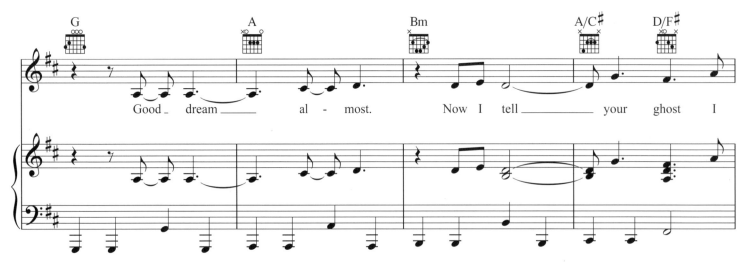

Good ___ dream ___ al - most. Now I tell ___ your ghost I

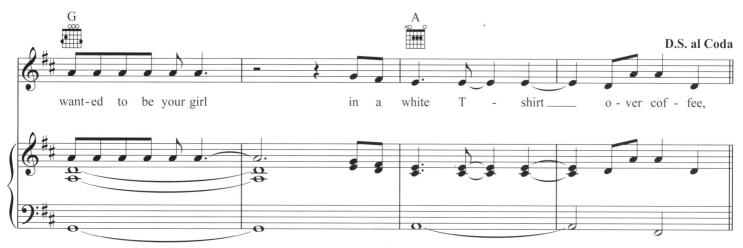

D.S. al Coda

want-ed to be your girl in a white T - shirt ___ o - ver cof - fee,

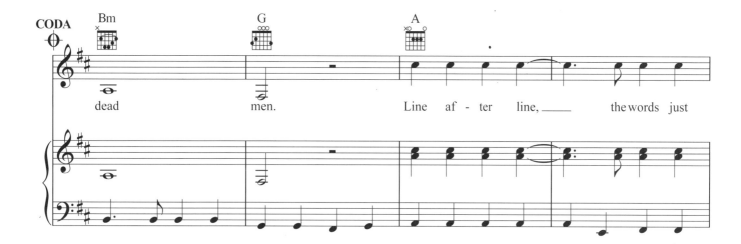

CODA

dead men. Line af - ter line, ___ the words just

serve to re - mind ___ two of us, oh, what we could have been,

po - et - ry by dead men. Fire ___ from em - bers ___ how can I

make you re-mem - ber? With a turn of a phrase, _____ would you

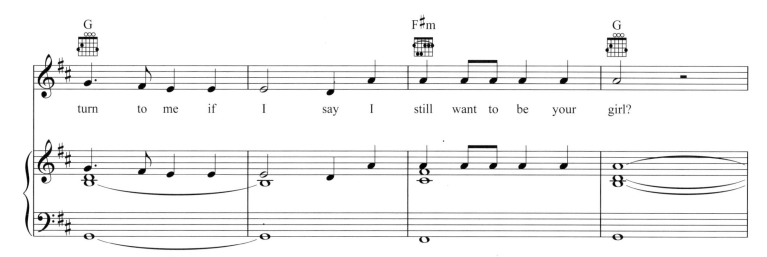

turn to me if I say I still want to be your girl?

I still want to be your girl ____ in a

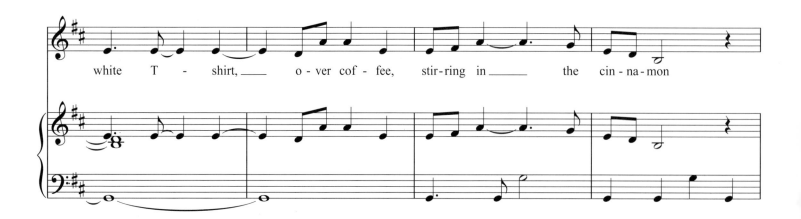

white T - shirt, ____ o - ver cof - fee, stir - ring in ____ the cin - na - mon

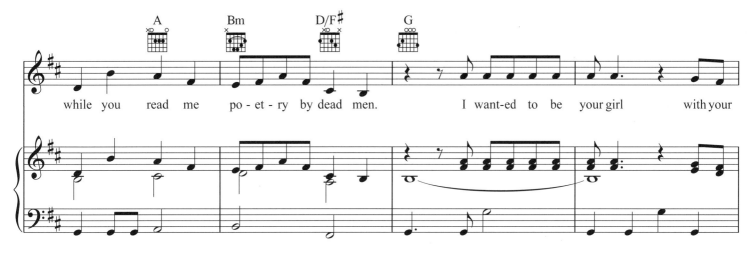

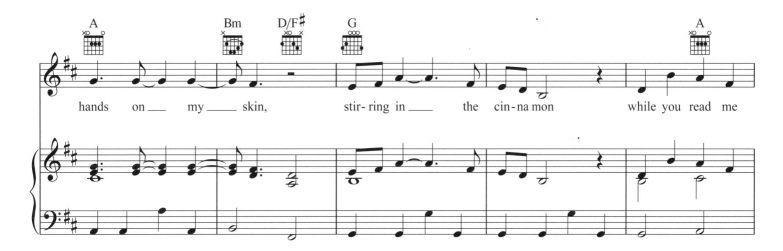

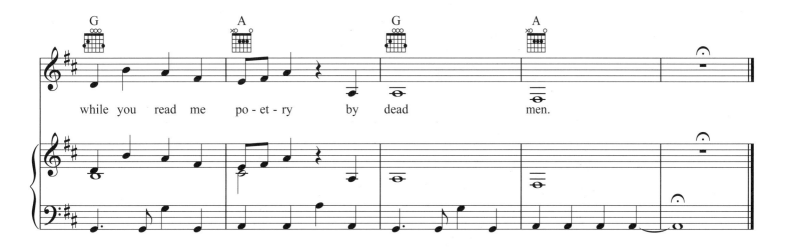

SOMEONE WHO LOVES ME

Words and Music by
SARA BAREILLES

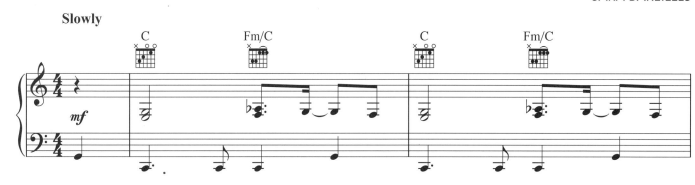

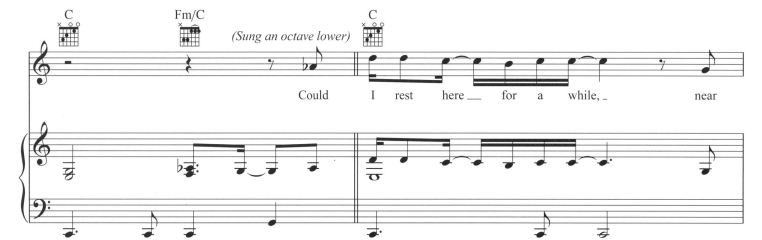

Could I rest here ___ for a while, ___ near that med - al 'round your neck?

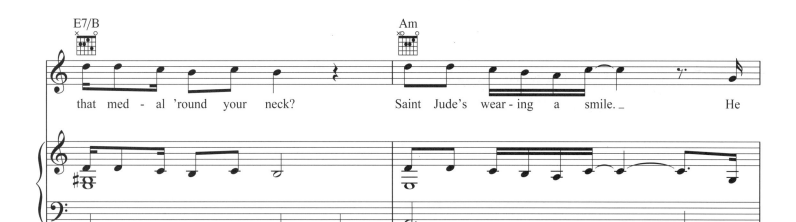

Saint Jude's wear - ing a smile. ___ He would-n't mind ___ I bet. ___

I ___ can't go face the world. ___ My

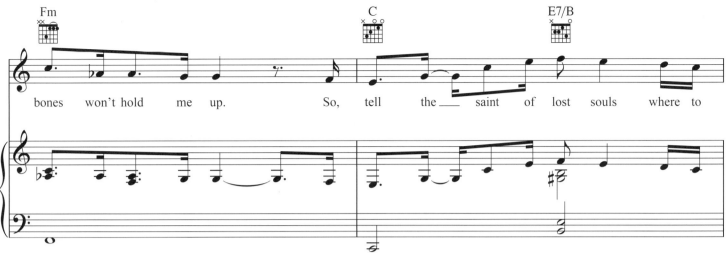

bones won't hold me up. So, tell the ___ saint of lost souls where to

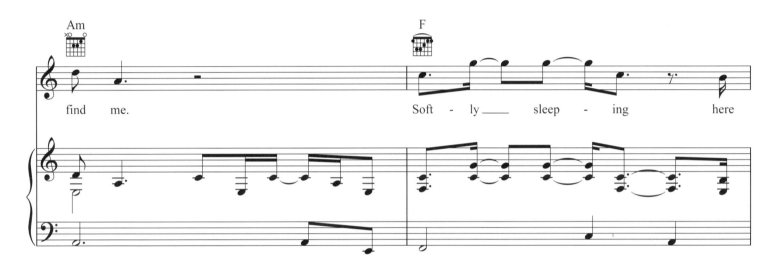

find me. Soft - ly ___ sleep - ing here

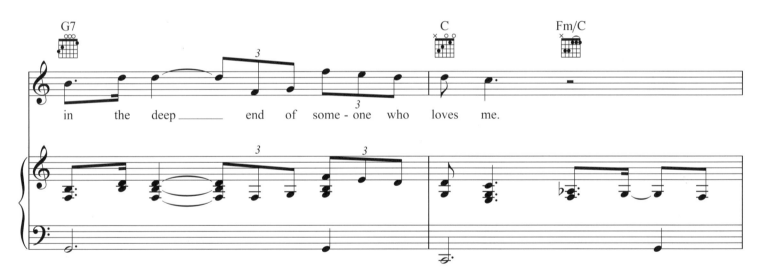

in the deep ___ end of some - one who loves me.

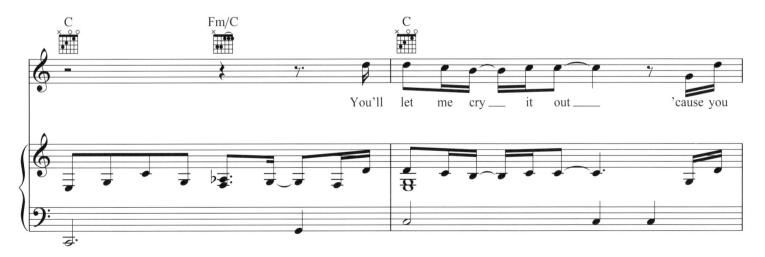

You'll let me cry ___ it out ___ 'cause you

know that some - times I can't stop and ___ still I'm seek - ing how to

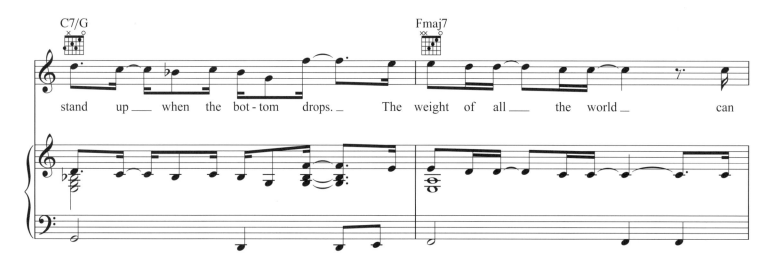

stand up ___ when the bot - tom drops. ___ The weight of all ___ the world ___ can

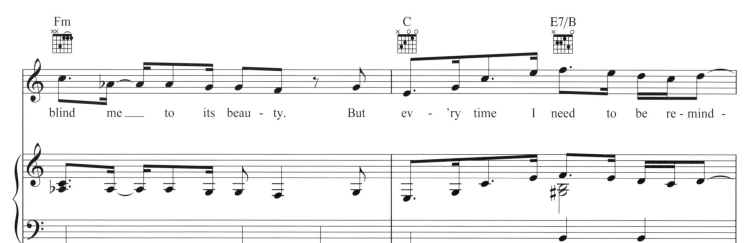

blind me ___ to its beau - ty. But ev - 'ry time I need to be re - mind -

- ed, I know you will and

say you're still ___ some-one who loves me. I ___

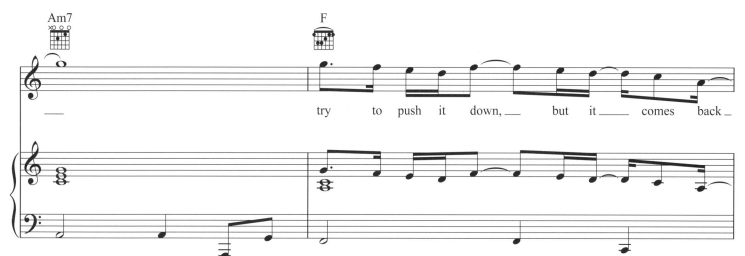

___ try to push it down, ___ but it ___ comes back ___

___ fast - er ___ and hard - er. ___

Tides _____ are chang - ing on a dime ___ and I'm ___ just try'n' ___

to keep my head a-bove the wa-ter. Sur-

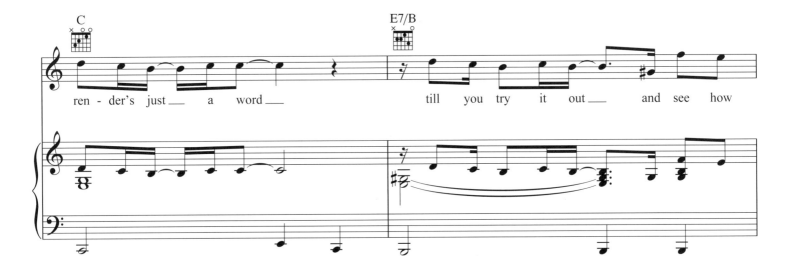

ren-der's just __ a word __ till you try it out __ and see how

hard it is to hurt __ with some-one else __ a-round. I'm the

worst I've ev-er been, __ a-fraid of __ al-most ev-'ry-thing. __ The

skies are clear, but storms are al - ways com - in'. ___ Your gift to me ___ is

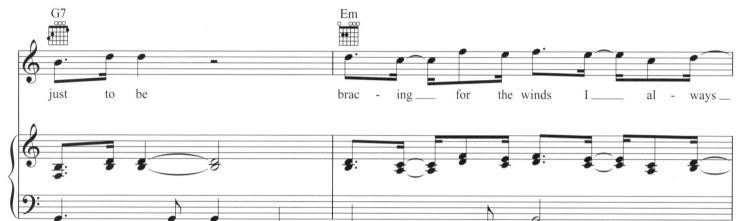

just to be ___ brac - ing ___ for the winds I ___ al - ways ___

___ sum - mon. _ My home, my heart, _ thank God you are ___ some - one who

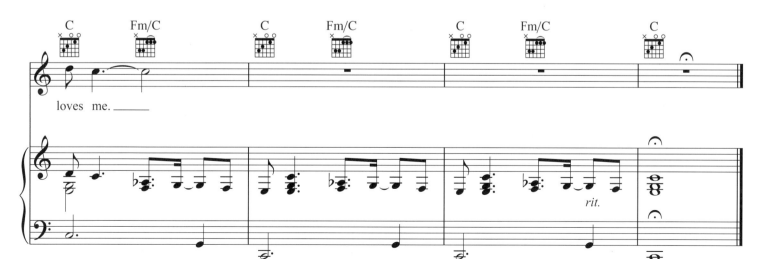

loves me. _____

A SAFE PLACE TO LAND

Words and Music by SARA BAREILLES
and LORI McKENNA

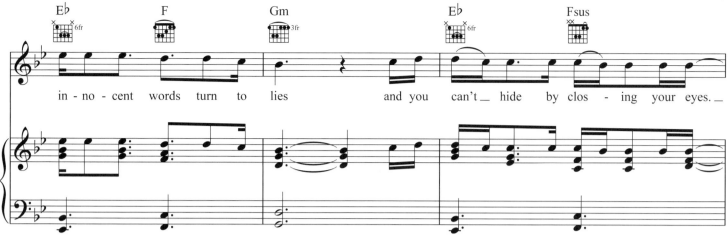

in - no - cent words turn to lies and you can't hide by clos - ing your eyes.

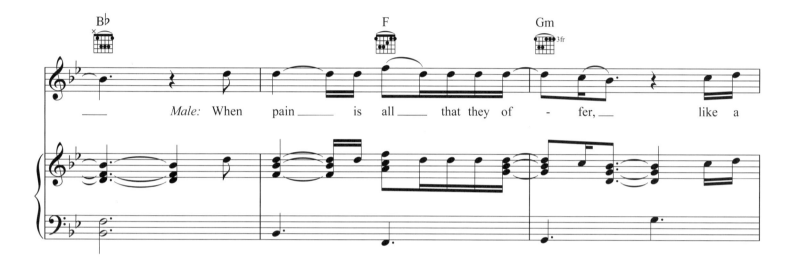

Male: When pain is all that they of - fer, like a

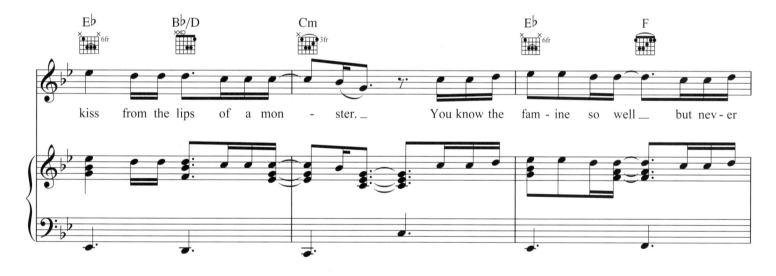

kiss from the lips of a mon - ster. You know the fam - ine so well but nev - er

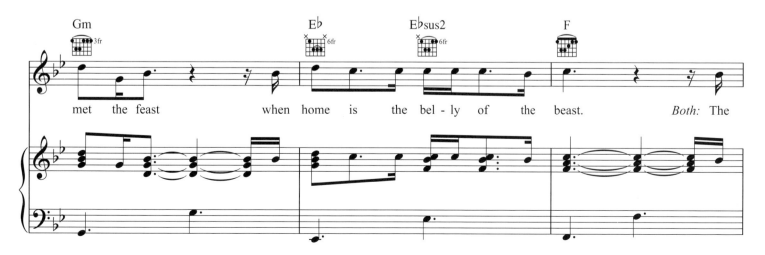

met the feast when home is the bel - ly of the beast. *Both:* The

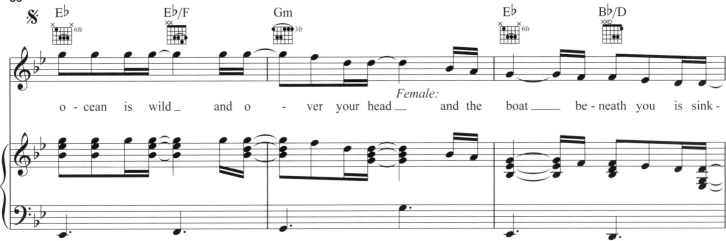

o - cean is wild ___ and o - ver your head ___ and the boat ___ be - neath you is sink-

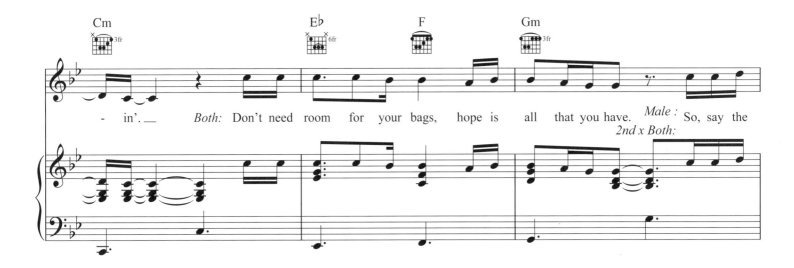

Female:

- in'. ___ *Both:* Don't need room for your bags, hope is all that you have. *Male :* So, say the
2nd x Both:

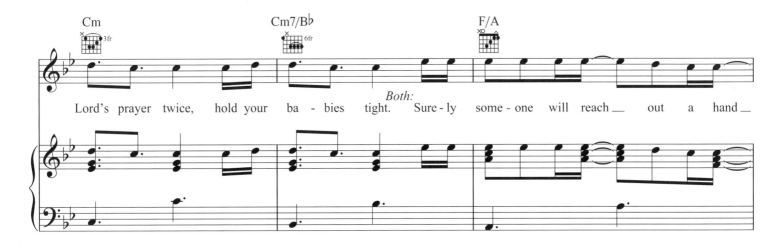

Both:

Lord's prayer twice, hold your ba - bies tight. Sure - ly some - one will reach ___ out a hand ___

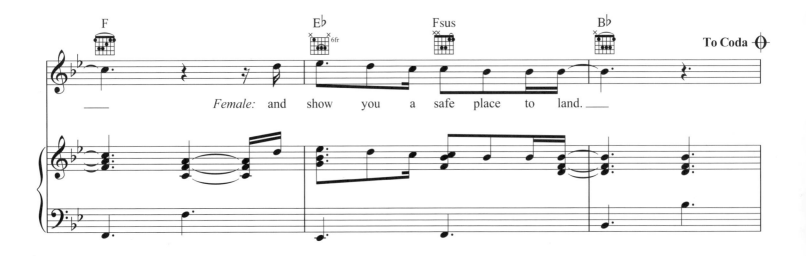

Female: and show you a safe place to land. ___

To Coda

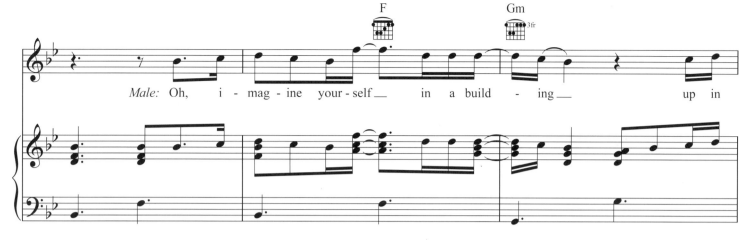

Male: Oh, i-mag-ine your-self __ in a build-ing __ up in

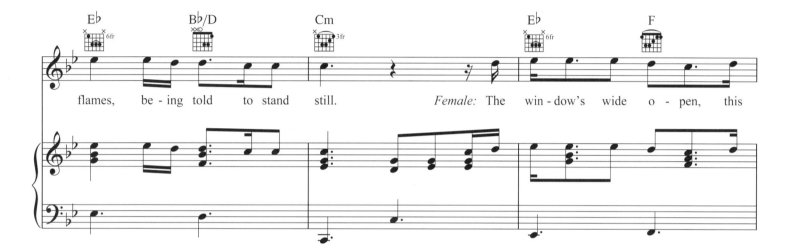

flames, be-ing told to stand still. *Female:* The win-dow's wide o-pen, this

Both: leap is on faith. You don't know who will catch __ you, may-be some-bod-y will. __ The

Both: Be the hand of a hope-ful stran-ger, lit-tle

scared but you're strong ___ e - nough. ___ Be the light in the dark of this dan - ger ___ 'til the

sun comes up. ___ Be the up, 'til the sun comes

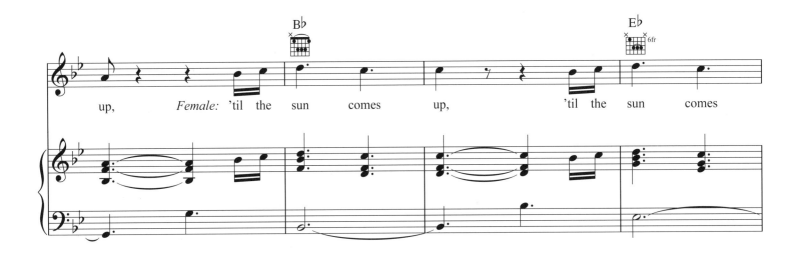

up, *Female:* 'til the sun comes up, 'til the sun comes

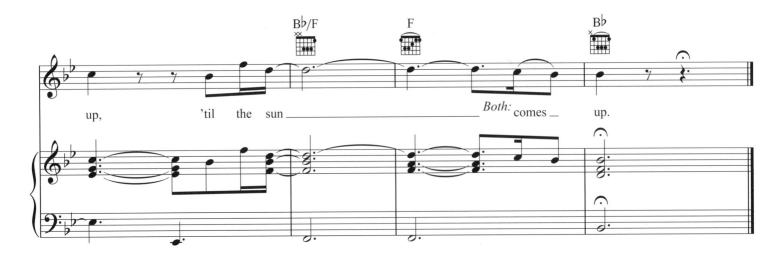

up, 'til the sun ___ *Both:* comes ___ up.